SCOTT MEMORIAL LIBRARY

DISCARDED FROM:
THOMAS JEFFERSON
UNIVERSITY LIBRARY

11-76

HEARTLAND

HEARTLAND

Mort Sahl

HBJ

Harcourt Brace Jovanovich
New York and London

Copyright © 1976 by Mort Sahl

All rights reserved. No part of this publication
may be reproduced or transmitted in any form or
by any means, electronic or mechanical, including
photocopy, recording, or any information storage
and retrieval system, without permission in
writing from the publisher.

Printed in the United States of America

Library of Congress Cataloging in Publication Data

Sahl, Mort.

   Heartland.
   1. Sahl, Mort.   I. Title.
PN2287.S22A34   791'.092'4   [B]   75-46551
ISBN 0-15-139820-8

First edition

B C D E

HEARTLAND

A week before he died, Adlai Stevenson asked me what was the worst problem. He answered his own question: There isn't anyone to talk to.

This is a book about the moment that concerned Joseph Conrad. When a man is born, a bullet is fired, his conscience—some will say his soul—and it ricochets off the events of his time until he is struck by it. That moment can be a shattering collision or an illumination. It is the time a man comprehends his purpose and his progress.

My experience is meaningless unless seen as a microcosm of America for ten years. Here is the pain and the ecstasy of a conscience out of control. It's not written in retrospect or triumph. It's a statement from the eye of the hurricane. It's a suspense story.

Those who think of me as an outlaw will realize that I think of myself as the sheriff. Whatever else you find, you'll know what side I'm on.

I started small. I didn't even run for President. Bertrand Russell said, "Conformity is death and protest is life."

Everybody wants to know where all the radicals have gone. If I serve any function, it is to raise questions and not to answer them. The question is: Where do the radicals come from? Dean Rusk wanted to know where Fidel Castro came from. Fidel Castro was a clean-shaven civil liberties attorney in a gray suit in downtown Havana until he couldn't stand it anymore. The established order builds the incubator for its overthrow.

All of this was the propellant for the guided missile that headed for the tranquil city of San Francisco on December 22, 1953. I was living in Los Angeles, and Los Angeles isn't like San Francisco; it is not a demanding love at all. L.A. is the other way: it is the girl you meet and have an affair with and then encounter at a cocktail party. The hostess introduces you to her and you are immediately filled with recognition of the events of the night before, but she shatters the ambience by thrusting out her gloved hand, saying, "How do you do," as she would to any stranger.

How did I get to San Francisco? Well, not by design—nothing is by design. It is nice to see yourself in terms of a hero. Most revolutionaries turn at a point that even they cannot recognize. They look back to the time when they altered their course, but the moment is not perceptible. It is never reached by design.

I was attending USC under the GI bill. It was a passive campus, except for the incident after the war when Helen Gahagan Douglas had come there during her race for the Senate and some of the supporters of her opponent, Richard Nixon, had spontaneously driven by in a truck, called her a "communist," and dramatized their passion by dousing her with red paint. Later, over coffee in the Student Union, one of these five activists on a campus of twenty-eight thousand told me he had been hired for this specific purpose by Murray Chotiner, who was Nixon's campaign architect and who cropped up later at the White House and would die, ostensibly of coronary thrombosis, on the sidewalk in front of Teddy Kennedy's home. We see here, for the first time, a thread of what is to become an elaborate embroidery.

I was taking a statistics course at Southern Cal. Well, how else can you document prejudice? The instructor was always emphasizing that Sigma was the symbol for the mean. One guy taking the course used to use his own initials instead of Sigma because his friends considered him the standard deviation. In anthropology, they taught us that the singular of "mores" was "mos," so, logically, it would follow that if habits were to become passé in this culture, one could assume that old man mos is dead. The irony is that intellectual humor, flowing freely, settles at the level of the pun. Well, back to the course.

One day I got to talking with a serious liberal—you know, the kind of guy who wanted to teach. That was twenty years ago; today he would be content to paraphrase Martin Luther King, Jr.—"I have a dream that someday every black man will have his own television series." Liberals went on to help Indians. John Ehrlichman suggested alternative service—he'd be a lawyer for Indians instead of going to jail. The Indians never needed a lawyer until they got a benefactor like Marlon Brando. Paul Ullmann, this liberal, said to me, "Do you still like jazz?" That's the impression I had made after several years of majoring in engineering. I could never wake up in the class, because I had been up all night making the rounds of the jazz joints, especially big bands and mostly Stan Kenton, who was my hero. His band had brass out to here! Most important, he was defiant. The band followed no rules except a greater allegiance than temporary popularity—the right of the artist to go his own way. I made it a point to meet Kenton. And later I knew why the jazz establishment was after him—the establishment, whatever the field it occupies, never objects to what you say, merely your opportunity to say it.

Ullmann told me that he'd met a girl and she was very fond of jazz, and because he was majoring in social work he didn't know where to take her when he was courting her. So he said, "I will get you a date with her girl friend, then we can double-date and you can take us to one of the jazz joints." I am basically a laissez faire capitalist, which means that even though I knew nine girls at that time, the idea of meeting another one had to be intriguing —in other words, nine businesses are bankrupt, so why not get a loan and start another one?

That night I was at the Palladium in Hollywood, watching the Kenton band, and I went to the telephone and called his girl to open liaison. I introduced myself, and although she knew the call was coming and she gave me her girl friend's number, she was also giving me the deep freeze (Barbara Walters on a cold day). Then I talked to her for thirty minutes instead of doing my homework, and I played social director and got everybody ready to go to a club called the Lighthouse in Hermosa Beach. So the next night Paul and I drove up to his girl friend's house and he said her name was Susan, and she was unforgettable, although as the story progresses you will see that I, not he, had the job of forgetting her. So, we walked in and met her, and she was just like she was on the phone —incommunicado. I met her parents. It was kind of a dream California home—upper middle class, Jewish, two girls.

We took off for the Lighthouse and started to talk about American jazz. I found myself in a closed conversation with Paul's girl, instead of mine, and it went on like that all evening. (This may sound tame, but America grew. When I went to New York in the '50's you had to be Jewish to get a girl. In the '60's you had to be black to get a girl, and now you have to be a girl to get a girl.) I was quite taken by this girl—at least I think I was. I hated school so much that I was taken by everything. I got to see more and more of Susan and found out that she was perfect. She was physically prepossessing, she was a leftist on the campus, she liked jazz, and she was an atheist. It certainly keeps your calendar filled up. I even remarked to a friend of mine, "I met a girl who is perfect; I can't seem to find a flaw." He said, "I know you and I have every confidence that you will."

One day she and I were parked out at Malibu, watching the grunion run, and I wondered how she had met

Paul, since he went to USC and she attended UCLA. She said, "I don't attend UCLA." I said, "You *are* a student, aren't you? What college do you go to?" She answered, "I don't go to college. I go to Los Angeles High School." I was twenty-three, and I asked, "How old are you?" and she said, "I'm as old as everybody else—I'm sixteen." So I said, "You're kidding." She said no and showed me her work permit from the employment bureau at school. So I said, "This isn't going to work, because I am twenty-three." She said, "So what? A lot of people are older than you are," which had not occurred to me at that point— it never does. So I said, "I think we have a problem." It's never like the movies. Out here on the street, "We're in love" is followed by "What'll we do?"

About this time she had to choose a college, which meant UCLA, about fourteen steps from her house. But she wanted to get away from her parents, and she did what all girls in west L.A. do when they want to get away: she chose to move to Berkeley, only a forty-five-minute plane ride, so the parents could go there at any time. She left for Berkeley just as I dropped out of graduate school after an explosive period with the Dean of the School of Public Administration at USC, Dr. Henry Rheining, who had given me a D on a term paper, attributing my failure to "emotional cathartics" because I had criticized the unification of the armed forces as essentially creating another branch—the Air Force.

I got a job in a car lot in south Los Angeles. Television was just becoming hot, and I had an arrangement whereby anybody who bought a television set at a certain appliance store would get a free automobile. I used to buy these cars in a junk yard, for $10 and $15, and I would charge the appliance store $25, so I would clear $10. The owner, who was Colin Kiggins, liked me. He used to drive a large Lincoln, and people were coming into the lot say-

ing, "I am entitled to a car and—" pointing to his Lincoln—
"I want that one." That may have been the moment I
became aware of the needs of the American people and
how they were not being met.

I was living in South Gate. My father had retired from
his twenty years with the federal government as a court
reporter and as an administrator with the FBI—yes, that's
right, the FBI—and was now doing administrative work
for the South Gate, California, Fire Department. He
wanted only to retire. He should have asked the Swedes.

To nourish my dreams, I used to hitchhike—because I
never had any money—into Hollywood and hang out with
Ed Penney and Dick Crenna. We were forever writing
plays, sketches, and radio programs, but the only one
who went to work was Dick, who was on radio on *A Date
with Judy* when we were all thirteen, and later progressed
to *Meet Corliss Archer, Our Miss Brooks, The Great
Gildersleeve*, and *The Real McCoys*. In fact, he worked
for thirteen years before I got my first job. In L.A. we had
attended Virgil Junior High School, Belmont High School,
and USC together. Appearing as a guest on my television
show in L.A. about ten years ago, Crenna said that I had
been antiauthoritarian since I was ten—authority included
my father, the principal, and the President—and he added
that he felt the administration could have spared itself
a lot of pain if it could have corrupted me early. "Mort
never told me he wanted a better world; he just said he
wanted a cowboy suit. If his mother had gotten him a
cowboy suit, then maybe Nixon wouldn't have been attacked by him for twenty years."

I hitchhiked to Berkeley to see if there was anything
outside. In many ways it was like being born again. A lot
of people miss the first time. Berkeley had three shifts of
people who were forever talking politics in coffeehouses.

There was a cadre of left-wing-oriented Jewish kids with fervor. I just wandered around and listened.

One of them was Armando Del Torto. He needed a place to live, so he took a job with a real estate firm, managing a five-hundred-room hotel because he got a free apartment, and everything went well until somebody asked him to change a light bulb, which he didn't know how to do. Later on they asked him to collect the rent, and he didn't want to do that on the principle that it was exploitation of working people. At a popular gathering point on the campus, the White Log Tavern, one guy held the record for eating donuts and drinking coffee for thirty-one days. He used to get up at night and circle the booths for exercise. The White Log got a turnover by not letting students use the men's room. But this guy so impressed the manager that they had unlocked the rest room for him —and that was how he set the thirty-one-day record.

Berkeley was a good place for L.A. girls to be liberated. They could form peace marches; they could forget their parents and pretend to be poor; and they could live with guys—which they could never do if they stayed at home. My relationship with Sue was like Chaplin's tramp with the rich man in *City Lights*. We were in love at Berkeley, but when she went home for Easter or Christmas, I would go over to her house and she would greet me in sweater sets and saddle shoes and talk to me through a surgical mask. (John Kennedy said Wayne Morse treated him with the same ambivalence.)

Economically, things were getting worse for me. I was living in the back of Del Torto's '36 Buick. He had progressed from his triumph as manager of the Hotel Ashby and was now the manager of a fast-food restaurant called

Doggie Diner. The place had no dishes, just paper wrappers. When you paid, they added up the wrappers—unless you had eaten one. When they closed at night, I ate whatever pie was left—apple pie, cherry pie, peach pie. Anyway, I was talking to Sue about writing and performing, and I was in my usual obdurate posture. Everybody was saying that audiences were stupid and I was denying it. I never felt any comfort in defining my fellow men as an alien group. It never made me feel secure. What security is there in knowing that if you hemorrhage, your fellow man has a different blood type? Somehow, I came to the point of believing that intelligent comedy can muster an audience. I was never called an intellectual myself then, although I am now called that. Once, when he left America, C. P. Snow said the United States is the only country where Dick Cavett could be considered an intellectual. Steve Allen was considered an intellectual in show business too. You hear it often: Cavett is more intelligent than Johnny Carson and Merv Griffin. It's like saying he is the smartest bear in the zoo.

Well, Sue and I were talking—to those who see me as a misogynist, I've always paid women the ultimate compliment, which is that I listened to them, whereas Schopenhauer said if women didn't have a unique anatomy there would be a bounty on them. I said I was going to try my hand at being a comedian. I didn't have the equipment. I didn't have a tuxedo. You needed that in 1953, and a line of girls behind you. She said, "Why don't you try out in this club in San Francisco? It's in North Beach, which is the bohemian area—which means a lot of Jewish people acting like Italians. Why don't you go to the hungry i?" She added, "The audiences are all intellects, which means if they understand you, great, and if they don't, they will never admit it because they will think it is whimsical humor." She had a beatific smile on her face that I had seen many times before when a counselor sent me out of the unemployment office in Los Angeles.

The hungry i was a cave under San Francisco with eighty-three benches seating eighty-three, illegal from the standpoint of the fire department because there was only one entrance and it was also the exit. They served a smorgasbord of lunch meat (remember that in school when you cursed your mother but you had no choice, you were poverty-stricken) and American cheese on white bread. I walked in and there was Enrico, who was Harry Banducci of Bakersfield, who was with his manager, Barry Drew. I gave them an audition, and when I got through he took me next door to a Chinese restaurant and said to me, "You look like you are starving, and even if you never work, here's $20." Then a call came through saying that Dorothy Baker, who was singing in the club, was going to take a day off and he said to me, "You can work that night." So I arranged to come back and work at the hungry i.

I went back to Berkeley and I asked all my friends to load the audience, which they did. I went back there with a cast-off coat and a tie that were given to me by some of Kenton's musicians. I couldn't remember my material, so I stapled it inside a newspaper. The audience laughed like hell, and I got the job for a week because Dorothy Baker, by that time, was leaving for Hollywood to marry Jack Brooks, the composer of "That's Amore."

I went on for a week and the audience—this time when I came back I didn't have my friends from Berkeley—booed and hollered because a strange face was uttering a strange philosophy without a dialect. An audience has to have a banister or they are going to fall down the stairs and take you with them. Boy, they were mad. They threw pennies at me—and peanuts onto the stage. They were really savage.

Enrico said, "Fire him." And Barry Drew said, "You give me all the dirty jobs; you do it." They argued for three months, and meanwhile I stayed. It was my first view of Enrico not wanting to make a decision as an executive, which was to happen for the next fifteen years. He would say, "Let him stay—we'll have three acts instead of two." We eventually had six acts on the bill because of that. He didn't want to be a heavy, or a nightclub owner, for that matter.

At the start I was either at the hungry i, on the stage, or across the street in a Chinese restaurant with a notebook, writing material like the cable car story, which was about the Christmas rush and a cable car conductor who gets ready for it. He's retired, but he's called out of retirement by the Rapid Transit District. He takes his mementos, which are two coin changers, off the wall, and as he straps them on, he says, "I never thought I'd have to put these on again." Well, the audience of course identified with motion pictures in those days.

Another story was about a bank. Two robbers walk up to an intellectual who can't get a job other than a teller's— that may be as true today as it was twenty years ago—and they hand him a note that says, "Give us all the money in the bank. Act normal. You will not be harmed." The teller returns the note with a counternote asking about the word "normal." He wrote, "Define your terms." College audiences loved that.

I worked from the newspaper headlines, and out of that came all the material about Eisenhower. Remember when Humphrey said that Eisenhower should take a black girl and walk her into a segregated school? I suggested that Eisenhower was having a terrible time deciding on how to do it, whether or not to use an overlapping grip. When Governor Faubus called out the National Guard to stop the school integration in Little Rock by the federal government, I said I liked Governor Faubus, but I wouldn't want him to marry my sister.

So-called intellectual humor caught on, and what is probably my biggest secret is that most Americans look down on other Americans and think they're the only ones that understand the act. All people understand the artist. People get varying degrees of understanding from an artist, but art doesn't leave anyone cold. More than political censorship, or any other kind of censorship, I ran into intellectual discrimination against the audience, which is the most dangerous censorship of all. I try to alleviate it as best I can. There's a lot one man can do, any man, but you can't do it alone. Hitler demonstrated that a lot of people had to march to start a war, but we know a few can march to stop one.

Once, I was standing in front of Stefanino's on the sidewalk, and Dean Martin says to me, "My daughter is going to college and thinks you are the best thing that ever happened." Twenty years later, he says, "You son-of-a-bitch" (affectionately, of course), "you got a trick up your sleeve: Whenever we throw you out of the house, you know the kids will bring you in the back door." Funny, when I said I was thrown out by the show business elite, it was called paranoia.

After I got started at the hungry i, I picked up my dad and my mother, and a U-Haul trailer, and I brought them to Sausalito and said, "Remember you said you would die at a desk at the fire department. . . . Well, that isn't going to happen, because you're retired." I didn't know that I had just declared war on their spirit. My father had a trunkful of papers in the back of a closet marked "Harry Sahl—personal." He was a modest man. When he died, I was to dig into that trunk and find his press clippings. He won several drama awards, including one for a play at the University of Denver. I found the work he had tried to

15

do on Broadway and the disappointments he had met. He was a lot like Arthur Miller in spirit—not the poet that Tennessee Williams was thought to be, but the analyst that Arthur Miller is. I preferred to see things in that prism. My dad was disappointed in his dreams and he distrusted that world for me, and it caused a great deal of conflict.

My mother was all enthusiasm. She picked up the paper and decided to write to "Mr. San Francisco." After I was eighteen weeks at the hungry i, Herb Caen walked in, attired in the wardrobe of the costume department—Brooks Brothers, a Pall Mall dangling from an aqua-filter—and with a blond model on his arm, the urban Jewish wit who was a columnist for thirty years in one town, heir apparent to Winchell, except that the empire was gone. He came in and he listened and he took me to dinner afterward and he said, "You are on your way." And from then on when somebody came to San Francisco, Herb Caen would show them the act at the hungry i, which was brought to his attention, he told me, by "some little old lady who didn't say her name." He brought in Eddie Cantor and he brought in Danny Kaye, and, finally, he brought in Harry Ackerman, president of the West Coast division of CBS Television. Ackerman signed me to a thirteen-week contract and he set it up with Phil Feldman, director of Business Affairs, to consummate it. We sat on two cases of J & B in the storeroom of the hungry i and went over a forty-eight-page contract, exchanging pens and initialing the riders. Feldman went on to produce *The Wild Bunch* with Sam Peckinpah, but at this time he looked at me and said, "Well, you're pretty intellectual. I am a graduate of the Harvard Business School myself, but I don't know if an audience will accept you." I came to hear that repeatedly during the years that followed.

When we first opened at the hungry i in San Francisco,

I used to do about fifteen minutes at a time and get out of the way. Since then, a lot of people think I've lost my discipline, and they say today, "Why does it take you an hour to cover a subject?" Believe it or not, its not me. It's that there wasn't that much wrong in the country then and you could cover it a lot quicker.

The Smothers Brothers were across the street at the Purple Onion and were the second act. One night the Smothers Brothers got laryngitis and they called me to tell me about it. I went over to do their shows. I had my shows to do and their shows. So I did fifteen minutes, then went across the street and did their show. I came back and did my show, and then I did their show, etc. At that time, North Beach was a place for a lot of conventions in San Francico. You know, four or five drunken guys and their wives walking around with those badges that say, THE NATIONAL PAINT AND CONCRETE FOUNDATION. HOWDY, I'M FRED. One night I was running back to the hungry i to do my third show and a couple of drunken guys lurched toward me, and one guy said, "Hey, kid, there's a guy at the other club using all your material."

Herb Caen stayed on Nob Hill, and Banducci was in North Beach. Herb Caen was encouraged by his wife, Sally, to get out and see how the other half lives. Herb had real dreams of glory. There wasn't one day when he'd give me a ride home that he wouldn't go up to Sacramento Street and look at the Union League Club with teeth clenched and say, "Someday I'm going to belong to that, Jewish or not." It's still there. He doesn't belong to it. And in that sense it's comforting to see that there are some things that don't change.

Caen's wife liked Sue, and Sue liked Sally. Very rarely do people get along on terms like that, and so we all went along. And then, eventually, Sue and I decided to get married and she told Sally, and Herb and Sally had us

17

marry in their house on Green and Scott in San Francisco before a lady judge. After the wedding we had a wedding breakfast at the Lochinvar Room of the Mark Hopkins, and I took off to go to work at the Sunset Auditorium in Carmel for disc jockey Jimmy Lyons. In the Bay Area they used to say, "You know, Dave Brubeck is God and Jimmy Lyons is his prophet."

Dave Brubeck's constituency had been growing at the Black Hawk, about a mile across town from the hungry i. Paul Desmond was then Brubeck's alto saxophonist, and unlike Brubeck, who had a wife and six kids and went home every night, Desmond was hanging out. He got to know me because I was in the public domain. I remember when we were doing a concert with Brubeck and we talked about the Sunset High School Auditorium in Carmel and the fact that Red Norvo had just recorded there and was looking for an album title. I suggested to Desmond they call it "Red Wails in the Sunset." It was Desmond's birthday, and I gave him a Rolex watch and it said on the back, "To the Sound from the Fury."

Brubeck and Desmond were quite a remarkable couple of guys. At one point they were so well attuned that they used to play interchangeable melodies while improvising. Desmond was a loner who looked upon me as some kind of misunderstood genius. He didn't understand how I could communicate. He told me that I would never realize what it is like to have to do it through a piece of bamboo. Outside of Stan Getz, Kenton, and Lennie Tristano, I don't know anybody I could listen to endlessly the way I did Brubeck. It was my custom, whenever I was on the road, to go wherever they might be and sit in with Desmond and Brubeck. I did the first college concerts with them, I guess in 1953.

So I had built my own ant village and these were the

people who fit into it. I was making my own people in
the lab—Enrico and Susan, and Desmond and Herb Caen.
We had a little circle. But the group in San Francisco,
they are a lot like Americans abroad, a colony, if you will,
who feed off each other. What did Physician Freud say?
We are an organism—we either grow or we decay.

After a year at the hungry i I was making close to
$1,000 a week, and a comedian came into Bimbo's, the
club in San Francisco, named Paul Gray. He came over
to see me and he liked me and said I should work in the
Black Orchid in Chicago. So I was signed and took off.
It was owned by Gertrude Niesen and her husband, Al
Greenfield. The manager was Benny Dunn, who now
delivers the movies on Sundays to Hefner's House.

When I got there I was wearing a sweater and they
said, "You don't have any class," which is something they
had expertise in, of course. They said, "You can't stay
in the club. You can do your shows, but you have to go
out on the sidewalk between shows," which I did. I had
to return through the kitchen, and I could not walk
through the club because I didn't wear a coat and a tie.
I quit and I went back to the hungry i for another year.

In the time I knew Enrico Banducci, which is a fifteen-
year run, he really was the only man who took a chance
on an unknown. And he had a certain flamboyance, which
created a business, but he couldn't run it. He had never
discovered anybody at the hungry i except me. I went to
the cover of *Time* magazine without ever leaving the
city of San Francisco, and I did it by having a one-night-
club platform. If you have a place to stand, you can move
the world. Consider what a television audience is by
numbers and then figure what it means to have only 265
people in a club. Yet everybody knew the hungry i, and
everybody knew that its connotation was Mort Sahl.

Later on, the club was identified with people I had sent there, like Shelley Berman, Jonathan Winters, Barbra Streisand, and Bill Cosby, but they all had been booked by theatrical agents.

Banducci also became a manager. There was a misleading side to him—both the front and the back. For instance, he would, before we went out to breakfast, go to the cigar box holding his evening receipts, grab about $500 and say, "This is for my son's college education—it's not as bad as it looks." In effect, Banducci was the symbol of the American Dream: I want to get mine.

Banducci finally got his opportunity. The hungry i was rebuilt twice. First he went from the eighty-three-seat cellar into a cellar across the street, for which he poured the concrete foundation and built the bar, by hand, and worked around the clock sandblasting. I used to finish the show and bring in the money in the cigar box from the small club, so that he could go ahead and pay for his building materials in the new club. I'd go in there in the middle of the night with coffee and donuts from Sai Yon's Restaurant in Chinatown to keep the guy going. He was sleeping on the concrete floor as he poured it—and then he'd get up and work some more, with an improvised gas mask of gauze over his mouth and nostrils.

I remember when he tore down a part of the wall underneath what was formerly a Chinese restaurant. He just sandblasted it, and when I walked in, it looked like the ruins of Frankfurt. I said, "What is the decor going to be?" He pointed to the scarred brick and the ashes and the mortar, and said, "That's it." And it was! Years later that would haunt me: whenever I would do a monologue—all the way to when I started my own show on the BBC in London—when I asked what the backdrop would be, they said, "There is only one set that connotes you to the public and that is a brick wall."

At the time of the Democratic primaries, Adlai Stevenson came to San Francisco. The NBC correspondent assigned was John Chancellor, who stopped me in Union Square and said, "Is there a good place to eat in town?" Thereby started the friendship. He introduced me to Jane Dick, who was head of women for Stevenson, and she introduced me to Governor Stevenson in Chicago.

The political nature of my material was beginning to emerge; the incubator was the lack of tolerance. I had said that the Army, having been called a communist bastion by McCarthy, had responded by redesigning the Eisenhower jacket. They added a flap that would go up over the mouth and called it the McCarthy jacket. I had said the Cold War, as defined, was that every time the Russians threw an American in jail, Nixon would throw an American in jail to make sure they didn't get away with it.

There was some resistance. As our club was literally subterranean, guys would come by and yell, "Communists," and other epithets, and would roll our garbage cans down from the sidewalk, down the steps, and through the door, and the momentum would make them lethal. Guys would wait upstairs to beat me up after work, and Enrico would walk out with me and take them on. He really did feel better when he had purpose, although he'd work like hell to look the other way. But when he was forced into action, he enjoyed it—and that was to become his dilemma with me. It was hard knowing me. I introduced him to Paul Newman. Once, when he went to pick up Newman at the airport, he said, "I love Mort." Newman said, "I love him too." And Enrico said, "But can you stand him twenty-four hours a day?" Newman said, "Hell, no."

21

In Chicago I went to Mister Kelly's and worked there for thirty-one weeks. When Mister Kelly's didn't have room for me because of previous bookings, I went downtown to the Blue Note, run by Frank Holzfein, a great jazz devotee. I worked with Maynard Ferguson and his orchestra, whom I dubbed "Twelve Angry Men." The entertainers stayed up all night. New York pretended to be open all night, and L.A. never was, but in Chicago you did your third show at four o'clock in the morning. I established the house record at Mister Kelly's. It's never been broken because no one else ever did four shows a night. Lenny Bruce was working in a place called the Gate of Horn, a folk singer's joint right behind Mister Kelly's.

Lenny was a product of Joe Maney's imagination. The debt to the humor of jazz musicians in general and Joe in particular was never paid by the moviemakers/mythmakers. Lenny translated with maniacal fidelity Joe's comic viewpoint. Joe was the original. And as for tragedy, Joe's end came in a game of real Russian roulette. No one else was playing.

Lenny was brought up before a Polish-Catholic judge. Lenny told him he was arrested because the judge was Polish and a Catholic—no diplomat he. And he argued with the police. One of the giveaways in Lenny's personality was revealed then. You know, he argued with one policeman about whether or not the officer's wife orally stimulated him. The policeman said, "You talk filthy." And Lenny said, "Well, if she doesn't, I feel sorry for you. Your marriage isn't complete." When he got into court, the judge asked Lenny, the great radical, that leader of heretics in American youth, what he thought was a complete marriage. Lenny said, "Oh, I like to wake up, and smell bacon cooking, and have my wife ironing over in the corner, and have her come over and fluff my pillow." How's that for a radical psyche?

But Lenny was of course not a radical. He was a master of colloquial triviality, and he has become what the *Wall Street Journal* called a metaphor for the liberals, and he remains something the self-serving liberals could seize upon, worshipers like Nat Hentoff, who once wrote irrelevant jazz articles and then went on to write bad political articles. You know, the kind who then equates civic virtue with how many Negroes are going to be motormen for the transit authority. Or Ralph Gleason, who spent his time lamenting the fact that Stan Kenton has no Negroes in his orchestra.

I used to kid about this on the stage and said that at the end of my act a lawyer came up from the audience and said, "Mr. Sahl, why don't you have any Negroes in your act?" And being a guilty liberal essentially, I ran out and hired one. Then I would look around me and say, "Well, you know these people haven't had opportunity for too long and their work habits aren't too good. For instance, this person I hired is not too punctual. I'm as liberal as the next guy, but you know I do have a business to run." And, of course, that always rang bells with the audience. Humor is the ultimate shorthand.

Every time the police would come in and record Lenny's act, and every time he'd swear, they would bust him. When he wanted money to get out on a writ, he'd call me. He was allowed one phone call, of course; so when he called he'd ask me to do the show, get some money from the owner, and come and bail him out. The police began to associate me with him in their minds, and they began recording me. They recorded me repeatedly, but they never did arrest me for obscenity. And that's because I'm puritanical, or, more likely, I never

met a cop who knew what the hell I was talking about.
You know, Hugh Hefner finally serialized Lenny Bruce's
book in the magazine. The title of the book was *How to
Talk Dirty and Influence People,* and, oddly enough, it
was a bomb. I don't think that any book in the history of
American publishing that was serialized ever failed to
have some sort of audience by the time it was pub-
lished in book form, with the exception of this one. In
retrospect, I believe that Lenny was funny when he was
a comedian, but he was wholly ignorant politically. He
used to say to me that he wondered why I found Stevenson preferable to Eisenhower, because, after all, they were
both hustlers.

Beyond that, Chicago was the home of Adlai Stevenson. In time Chicago would be known only as the home
of Hugh Hefner. It's weird the way things "develop." (I
think that's the word they use nowadays. Organic word.)
It's like going from Jefferson's saying "Resistance to
tyrants is obedience to God" to Richard Nixon's saying
"I am not a crook."

One night at Mister Kelly's, Hefner came in and we
met. His companion was Victor Lownes, the Third. My
God, are there two more? Playwright Herb Gardner once
said, "Lownes has the expression of a man who has a
season ticket to the end of the world." I always thought
Lownes most admired James Bond, the only man success-
fully to take fascism and make it a personal experience.
If you think that's bad superimposed on a whole people,
imagine it on a one-to-one basis.

Hefner told how he had borrowed $500 from his mother
to put out the first *Playboy* at the same time that I was
starting at the hungry i. And, like everybody I met in
those years, he claimed to be my blood brother. Sinatra
used to say it too. "We're both rebels." Hefner lived in an
apartment next to his office, and he had sun lamps in the

ceiling over his bed. And in this alcove, next to his desk, he would dress to go out at night. I used to come by after my show at three in the morning to pick him up. By then he'd be ready to go prowling. He'd ask me about mores. He said to me, "The magazine has got to do what you do. You make the people feel hip. I don't think that they are. I want people to feel like playboys for the forty-five minutes they scan the magazine. With that, I'll be satisfied." Hefner asked me who was styling hair in California, did people really invest in stereo sets, what was a bohemian, what was San Francisco like, and what kind of car did hip guys drive. I talked him into buying his first Lincoln and then, after that, in 1959, I told him to get a 300 SL. He got the Mercedes roadster that is still parked in his basement in the mansion in Chicago. Pretty cherry—about twelve miles on it.

Hef never ate—twenty years I've been waiting for him to go to dinner. He eats Franco-American spaghetti from the can. He likes hot beef sandwiches if he's at a banquet. And most of the time he has next to his bed the forty Pepsis he consumes in twenty-four hours, plus Twinkies and Heath bars. He used to comb Vitalis through his hair, turn to me, and say, "Are you still seeing Phyllis Kirk in California?" And I'd say yes. He'd say, "While you sow the seeds of your own destruction, why do the girls you choose have to be so bright?" That time was the height of race-relations movies, and I was going to make a movie called *I Passed for Bright*. And Hef said, "You got a choice. You can either be in love and be vulnerable, or make my decision to never know love and therefore be able to stand outside and solidly manipulate the relationship." He said that with a straight face.

The irony of Hefner is that his life is a suspense story only to him. It's all over but the doubting. It's predictable, of course, that a shy man should merchandise anticipation of pleasure—with no delivery date. He tells you it's all play but he was a businessman worried about circulation. In fact, when I listened to him at a staff meeting, I couldn't decide what business he was in. Maybe he couldn't either. Why else did he stay up for months at a time typing "the Playboy philosophy," as he did in a room next to mine at the Playboy mansion in Chicago. I mean literally months on Dexedrine, day and night, typing this *tome*. And for all he tells you to be a swinger, for the twenty years I knew him he had been close to only three girls, and maybe really only one. Her name was Mary Warren.

On the Playboy philosophy: no matter how much they insisted that they enjoyed living it up at Playboy, they didn't enjoy it as much as watching someone else attempt to. And when Hefner built the mansion, I had the feeling the first things that went in were the mirrors. They could watch how inept others were in the other rooms. He used to run stag films downstairs, which he turned off the minute I came into the house.

I used to come from Mister Kelly's back to the womb. The house was like the womb. It had a twenty-four-hour kitchen. It was designed so that Hefner would never have to leave. He left three times in two years, to see Tony Bennett, me, and the dentist. The dentist wouldn't come to the house. Total room service. Thirty butlers bringing you anything you wanted. Custom food in your bedroom, twenty-four hours a day. CinemaScope movies, closed-circuit telecast in the living room or punched in through your television set in your room. Ampex tape room with all the shows taped, in case you didn't want to watch them while they were on the air live. Bowling alley, a gymnasium, swimming pool. And, as they used to say, hot and cold running bunnies.

Hefner claims he printed, although he'd been warned,

the nude picture of Marilyn Monroe. As a result he was called in and given a fine, and throughout the hearing he beamed because he knew it tripled his circulation. America had its dream. The permissive generation had not yet arrived, and so a generation of the repressed found that for seventy-five cents they could look at a picture of a girl with a staple through her navel. It was a long way from Jean Arthur and Katharine Hepburn (and for those of us who thought that one day we would take her hand and walk off into the sunset) to paying seventy-five cents to look at a picture of a cheerleader.

Hefner never did discriminate. He was very fond of celebrities and, I suppose more than anything, he always wanted to be one. As his vision of the American dream, he accepted everybody who made a lot of money, the very people who would, he thought, come together at the country club at the end of the third act. He never realized that one of the privileges of position is to discriminate and to decide whose elbows you will rub. He never understood that. Doesn't today. But, like so many people who had fancied me, when I fell into or out of favor nationally he reported to me that it was hard to be my friend. He didn't realize that I had been on campuses where the most common question put to a person who espoused virtue was, "How do you explain your relationship with Hefner?" I had to defend myself. He had no idea that the next generation rejected him, ridiculed him. Of all the questions I heard, none was about sex; instead, they asked about the draft, the assassination, all the things that threaten living. After all, isn't it really life against death?

When he became more and more star-struck and eventually moved into Hollywood, my wife, China, said, "He's gone Hollywood after Hollywood was gone"—but I accepted Hefner for what he was. I was his friend.

After the Kennedy assassination, when I became involved with Garrison in the investigation of Clay Shaw, Hefner agreed to print an interview with Garrison, which I arranged. It was one of *Playboy*'s best-selling issues. When Clay Shaw was acquitted, Hefner ridiculed Garrison and had very little to say to me. I said, "Do you know why I'm not working?" And he said, "Well, you know, careers go up and down." And I said, "You're very cavalier about my adversity. Someday we'll see how you are about your own."

Still, he really thought I was the all-American authority. He was in California one day and a writer came up with a story that I thought was a natural for Hefner's new motion picture division. So I called. And his secretary, Bobbi Arnstein, picked up the phone and she said, "What's it about?" And I said, "I'd rather talk to him." So she said, "Well, he's very busy and if he gave every friend of his a handout—" He never called me.

Then I went to Chicago, and when I got up on the stage some girl yelled from the audience, "Hefner is a female oppressor," and I said, "Well, actually he's a male oppressor, but in actuality he's irrelevant." It was printed in the paper. Soon his chauffeur came over in a $42,000 car (a one-block ride) and handed a special delivery to me from Hefner, in which he said, "I understand you've taken to ridiculing me on the stage now, and I'm really wondering what that twenty-year friendship was."

So I called up and I said to whoever answered, "Listen, where's Hefner?" That night a call came through. "Mort?" And I said, "Yeah, who's this?" And he said, "Hugh Hefner." I said, "Listen, I think we'd better talk." So he said, "All right." And I went over to his house about seven o'clock with my wife. His secretary was on the floor, filing pictures. He was in his bathrobe.

I said, "Don't you ever use the word 'handout' with me." And he said, "Well, there's what people say and the way people hear it. People are afraid to tell you what they really think." I said, "I've noticed the fear, but I don't know the basis." "Well," he said, "there's a word." I said, "Go ahead." He said, "Paranoia." I said, "With the killings you see in the street? And with the fact that no election has been decided except by gunfire for fourteen years, you use the word 'paranoia'?" So he said, "Well, I don't know anything about political principles. I only have one thing in mind. You cannot leave this room unless you leave as a friend of mine."

As he raised his head I saw tears running down his cheeks. It was a jarring moment for China and me because we had no experience of this man ever revealing emotional ties.

It's different with Stan Kenton. We see each other maybe once a year, at which time (he's six foot five) he picks me up and kisses me. I've never been embarrassed by that. He can walk into an audience of twenty thousand and pick me out. We know each other on a special level. We agree on nothing; but, you see, you've got to get to the humanness.

In Los Angeles and New York, people take out their credentials. "Look, I'm with Nader's Raiders," "Look, I'm in the ACLU." It meant more to me when I went into Wallace headquarters and a campaign worker, this young lady, said to me, "Have you had dinner yet?" That plain humanity doesn't exist with the liberals. They've forgotten who they are.

All that was later. During the early days of my traveling, my wife was going to college in Berkeley and then to San Francisco State College. She was in graduate school, studying psychology. She was going to help people. She was always in school, and when I took off to go on the road to spread my wings, she was not available. She wasn't available when I came back either. I wondered why she was not at the airport. She said to me, "Well, I'm a person too."

I was driving a lot to Los Angeles. I had signed a contract with CBS. It was their habit to have me come down to Los Angeles every Monday to discuss my career. During the thirteen weeks I was with them, I never worked for them. The same thing happened to me later when I was signed by NBC. I never worked for them except to be loaned out to CBS, incredibly, for the *Ed Sullivan Show*. So I'd drive to Los Angeles.

I was tireless in those days. Like all young performers, I didn't know the meaning of "economy." That's pretty depressing about performers. I find that in Las Vegas nowadays they're on an hour and a half and they turn around to the orchestra leaders and yell, "One more time, Maestro!" I mean, that's hard to believe, if you transpose it. When the whistle blows for the end of the day shift at the Ford factory, does a welder say, "Please, let me make three more Pintos"?

I'd arrive at Television City in Hollywood, after driving all that distance, to check into a motel, take a shower, and run over to the studio. Then I'd drive back to San Francisco to work at the hungry i until two o'clock in the morning.

At that time there was a noontime show called *Club 15*. The two writers who were assigned to develop me, Bernie Gould and Paul Harrison, would talk to me. First, William Dozier, the head of the network, would talk to me and tell me I was too intellectual for most people, which I thought was in-depth analysis. Dozier's last contribution to television was *Batman*, but that's not to say those are his limits, which may be the most damning evidence of all. He's a very bright guy, but, oh, boy, that cynicism!

He'd like to do good things but he doesn't think anybody is as intelligent as he. I always got along well with him, and I stood by him, speaking at every farewell dinner whenever he left a studio. His people hated to see him go, enough so that they had a luncheon in his honor a block from the studio, from twelve o'clock to one. They all looked at their watches, wiped away a tear, and went back to work under the new boss.

At Television City, I'd leave Dozier and then I'd talk to Ackerman, head of programming. Then I'd go down with Gould and Harrison and do the warm-up for the *Club 15* show. Can you imagine that? Here came these women off the bus from having seen *Breakfast in Hollywood*. I would go out and do the warm-up before noon! Can you imagine what I said standing there in that sweater? But I did it. Yet the networks still said they just couldn't get a handle on what I did; it was too intelligent.

So I would then go back to San Francisco with renewed vigor because it was great to have your own platform. I'd walk into the hungry i, and I was a hero. And somehow it was never too intelligent for them. I found out, I guess, what teachers feel like. You know, it's not a democracy, a school. And if you owe anything to the students, it's to uplift them, to make knowledge attractive. If you leave it to them, they're going to say, "On a democratic basis, we prefer recess and chocolate milk."

We were now at a point at the hungry i where we did five shows on weekend nights. I wound up twenty-five minutes for the hour, five times a night. People were sitting everywhere, on the piano, on the stage. They couldn't get enough. It was fatiguing, but it was the best kind of tired I've ever experienced. I used to sit up all night with Enrico after the show and he'd say to me, "Someday you're going to make $7,000 a week and I'm going to pay it to you and I'm going to make money off it." I thought, My God, where are the men in the white coats? Take this guy away while he's still harmless. But he was right; he had tremendous vision, even though he measured the closest distance between two points via a corkscrew. It's not that he didn't mean what he said; it's just that he forgot fast.

We were making so much money at the club that Hollywood got wind of it, and we began to be visited by the agents. All the smart guys came in from MCA and the William Morris Agency. You now William Morris from television—"When I drop this tablet into water, thousands of tiny agents go to work." Every agent would walk up and say the same thing to me: "I don't think the average man will understand you." So, they didn't want to sign me. They said they didn't want to threaten the audience.

I ran into that attitude repeatedly and still do. To characterize the audience as stupid serves the purposes of the Johnny Carsons, because if it were established that the audience didn't accept pap, how would he fill the order? Where would he be? He is an anesthetist. In fact, Johnny Carson is Prince Valium. It's much like Dorothy Parker. She was once screening an inferior movie and somebody said, "Why do the writers prostitute themselves; why don't they give the best they're capable of?" Dorothy Parker gesticulated toward the screen and said, "They do, and that's it."

The hungry i was rapidly becoming the intellectual's way station, and everybody would drop in to see us. Walter Cronkite would be coming through San Francisco, and he'd hang out and drink with us every night. John Chancellor would come back again and again. All the movie actors would be in town. Franchot Tone was in town doing a play. Burgess Meredith came in; and he's the one whom Enrico originally contracted as an investor.

He was doing *Teahouse of the August Moon* at the Geary Theater. They'd all come down to the club every night.

One night I remember I had just come back from CBS, and I couldn't believe the network had said my thirteen weeks were up; they didn't know what to do with me. Phil Feldman of CBS suggested that I give them another thirteen weeks to decide, but go off salary. So it became a confrontation. I came back and was really depressed that they had no more confidence than that.

Franchot Tone said to me, "You are an enigma because everything you tell us in general that we accept on the stage, you yourself cannot accept in the specific. You're naïve, you're a child." And I thought about what he said all night. I guess it's true. You know anti-Semitism exists, and then you run into it once more. It's cold water right in the face. But maybe that's my whole story; I cannot reconcile myself to the inevitable.

If my father said to me that show business is not available to me because of my station or my limited abilities or the economics or whatever, I'd feel that if my passion was contaminated by reason, anybody's reason, I was in mortal danger. I had to continue to dream. Many people have appointed themselves that sacred charge—the killers of the dream. If somebody suggested that the audience was not intelligent, I thought that was the ultimate discrimination, rather than to call them Negroes or Jews or regionally ignorant or whatever. It's the ultimate discrimination—to say that all people are intellectually inferior, to place a ceiling on them. My God, I felt that had to be contested and fought down to the wire. The wire might become a garrote, and you might need to use it, depending on how crucial the stakes.

What does that mean—you cannot accept the inevitable? Do you fight the overwhelming forces and do you prevail? Maybe not, maybe you're never in the majority.

Maybe your position will change again and again, but your role never will. Maybe you're never acquitted, you're eternally condemned. Maybe you just get a stay of execution.

Dylan Thomas said you must rage against the dying of the light. Well, first you have to be offended by it. All my life I've heard people say, "Well, those are the conditions that prevail; you have to live with it." One day they asked me to live with assassination. It's elementary algebra: I don't think you can live with murder; it isn't idealism, it's functionalism. And it doesn't allow for the liberal thesis of coexistence. Let me tell you, the killers are not interested in coexisting.

Jazz musicians were saying that, as Lennie Tristano put it, my newspaper was my ax and I improvised within a chord structure, which was my thematic material. They felt a natural affinity with me, and I with them. I had started to write a column for *Metronome Magazine,* which was a sister publication of *Downbeat* at the time, and had been able to underscore my alliance with jazz. In jazz clubs they seemed to know that what I had to say was innovative in the same sense that Marlon Brando's work was at that time. Marlene Dietrich said to me once in 1957, "Brando's secret is that he acts like a human being, and most actors act like actors." Well, I acted like a human being and talked about those things that affect human beings, rather than talked like a nightclub comedian. My secret was in the public domain—that the audience has just as great a stake in what happens to America as I do. I believe that, and I bet my life on it.

Most comedians can never bring themselves to do that. They come in contact with the audience just long enough to pick its pockets; they hope to join the establishment. Shelley Berman said to me, "I'm no hero; I'm what you call a social democrat." He said it on my program in 1966 in Los Angeles. "I don't want to make waves." When Irv Kupcinet asked Allen and Rossi on his program in Chicago, "Do you think actors should get into politics," in a reference to Ronald Reagan, they indicated it could be fatal; look what happened to Mort Sahl.

If you ask them what happened to Mort Sahl, they'll say nothing. They'll give you the elaborate fable subscribed to by Steve Allen, Hugh Hefner, and Johnny Carson—that I bored the audience to death. It's a bum rap. My romance is with the audience.

My access to the audience was eroded by people who can control that access when I threw everything to the wind and said, "America's in trouble, and that's my priority." I knew that the fight had gone out of this family. The fight goes when the purpose goes. If the government can say to the American people, "We're not anticommunist anymore; it's not politic," and if the American people can then feel deprived of its purpose, they're made for each other.

A friend of mine says that God made us for this moment. Well, there is a confluence of events, and I think what distinguishes a man is how he acts when he reaches the intersections of history where collisions occur. You're a witness. Do you run away or do you report the accident faithfully?

I made the first comedy record in America, and although I hadn't bargained for much more than telling jokes in San Francisco and racing sports cars, believe me, I was very much an American. It was a challenge to me personally to reduce the complexity of Detroit or Bell & Howell or whoever to my own needs. I really liked all that. I like measuring distance, covering it, determining where I was, navigating across the alien planet, and trusting my fate to the stars.

I was the first nonmusician to work all those jazz festivals, and being accepted, the first comedian to cut a popular record, and probably the first man to integrate musical groups on the network. But I think you lead your life and those are the by-products, because you don't originate things. What you do is you renew what was good in the past. America doesn't need a social critic; it *demands* one.

When Susan and I got married, it was a shock to her family. For those of you who appreciate soap opera, her father was a grocer who had had two young daughters during World War II—an ideal situation. When I met her, he thought I was a bum. I wanted to get into show business. He thought I was a dreamer. To his utter amazement, here I was in show business, or, as he put it, "We never knew you'd become Mort Sahl." True stories are the funniest, and I hope to include all of them without mercy. Because you don't need mercy. You need justice. The Christians confuse you with mercy. The Jews want to bring you justice.

I remember my father-in-law saying to me, "You don't dislike money so much now that you're earning it, do you?" I like people who talk in sentences like that. It doesn't leave you with any empty spaces that you have to fill in with an answer. His attitude was, "Here we are in Auschwitz, Mort. The guards are decent guys, but every time you try to escape, they have to beat us up." I never had an answer for him anyway. I had this involuntary reaction: I wanted to punch him all the time. But I didn't know what that would prove. Anyway, there's always some kind of tolerance toward your enemies. That civility usually stems from the fact that you've married your enemy's daughter.

We were married. We had our misunderstandings. We

would have broken up except for the children. Who were the children? Well, she and I were. We got a divorce. We were married two years, seven months, and twenty days—the number of hours escapes me at the moment. No, we both escaped, speaking of escape. After it was over, she went back to school to study psychology, which she did for almost twenty years. (I don't know how one can be a perpetual graduate student. It reminds me of the prison warden who once told the International News Service that he became a prison guard, and eventually a warden, and he made that his life's work because he liked people.) Of course, I know that there are those of you out there who are going to say, "Well, I've seen people helped by psychology." I've seen cannibals helped by Christianity. Listen, it's really endless.

I was at the point where I was working at the hungry i a year, a year and a half at a time. In 1957, which of course meant I was changing the material—twenty or thirty minutes' worth—every two weeks or so, it came to me that every time I read a newspaper it went through a distillation process. Artistically, my modus operandi was not to rehearse. But in another sense I was always preparing. I was playing back the sounds of my time. People were listening to me. They believed me. And later on I was to test that, as we shall see very soon.

I started the end of 1953, Christmas. But around 1957, when I got to Chicago, a lot of comedians were coming out of the shadows, because I was showing them it wasn't as cold in the light as they feared. Shelley Berman approached me, and then Mike Nichols and Elaine May came, and Bob Newhart, and Jonathan Winters was in New York when I arrived there. Most of the comedians came out of "improvisational" theater, and they all still use that word.

I've never used that word, and I've never written a syllable except on the stage. I rehearse in front of the audience. Not because I'm daring or a practitioner of Russian roulette, but because I don't know how to write it on a typewriter. It's like rehearsing a conversation. Most people who call themselves comedy writers are no more than a card file. How many television shows have I done where a guy arrives and calls himself a writer for the show and then feeds back to me what he heard off one of my record albums. It seems to me that a lot of comedians collectively develop cabaret theater sketch material and then each leaves and claims it as his own. David Steinberg is from that group too; but he and Woody Allen are dangerous because they represent the degeneration of the Jew as a social force. To go from John Garfield to Woody Allen is putting in a lot of Clorox.

First, Berman came to Mister Kelly's and sat every night and told me of his high hopes to alter American comedy. And I got him the contract at Verve Records, and I put him in the hungry i, and I put him in Basin Street in New York, and I never saw him again. He became America's problem, and that's OK with me, because he got to a point where he was making $22,500 a week at the Sahara Hotel in Las Vegas and all he wanted to be was Red Skelton. Some revolutionary.

I've stood on the stage for twenty-one years now and accosted the President and the Chief Justice. But I've never held myself up to public scrutiny. And no one's ever questioned my credentials except as a comedian. They accept me as a senator at large. It's quite incredible when you think about it. That's one thing with my humor. I demand that you think about it, even if you don't laugh about it. Professional humorist is a misnomer anyway. The greatest wit I've seen exhibited in this country was a by-product of intellect, as in Adlai Stevenson, Eugene McCarthy, and John Kennedy. If you listen to the comedians, you can't even tell what point we are at in our chronological history.

About two years ago, I watched *The Tonight Show* one night and Johnny Carson referred to the War, and Don Rickles said, "Do you mean World War II?" Vietnam hadn't made a lasting impression; it had only gone on for twelve years.

Professional comedians, surprisingly, have a lack of humor. They're insensitive to the insanity of our times. America is bedlam at this time, and the only thing that makes the agony bearable is humor. There's nothing that can't be kidded about. You can set your own outside limits and you can edit yourself. You can joke about anything. I know; I've had some pretty good challenges. I've taken the entire Warren Report on the stage, read parts to the audience verbatim, and joked from there. I found a way to do it. It took me a while, but I found a way. If you don't have the skill to make the target humorous, you don't have the right to the audience's time.

If it comes down to whether one comedian or another has an annuity, I say, what is the difference? Most of them are very dedicated to retiring our time. You know, I think it's very significant in television that when they go on the air, they start the clock at sixty on an hour show. When the directors check with the girls, they'll say, "How much time have we got to go? How much have we got to kill?" Television is a product of our time; it glosses and it doesn't quite cover the subject. It flirts with ideas and it has no fidelity to them. What was it that Humphrey used to say? "I'm not necessarily wed to that concept." I used to think to myself, You're not even faithful to it. English is a blessing. One of the great tools comedians don't work with is the English language.

Something was stirring in the late '50's in America even if people couldn't define it. Paul Desmond got in touch

with me one day about George Wein, who owned Storyville in Boston and who, in his physique, resembled a
grinning bullet. He said, "Wein runs the Newport Jazz
Festival and has heard about you, and musicians love you,
etc. Why don't you come back and work Storyville with
us." So I figured, Well, it's time to leave the womb. I'm
going to go to Boston.

I was introduced during that engagement to the Boston
culture, which was tremendously jazz oriented. There was
a jazz dentist everybody went to, and of course Father
Norman J. O'Connor, S.J., who was the jazz priest. I got
daggers from him from the beginning, I think, not because
I strongly question organized religion, but who the hell
organizes it. The giveaway is that a Catholic priest would
resent what I said about Billy Graham. You see, when
the chips are down, he and Billy are on the same side. You
might say they're on God's side. But I never heard God
say that.

While I was working at Storyville, Duke Ellington
arrived to do a concert at Symphony Hall promoted by
George Wein. It was winter in Boston, which can be pretty
grim. So they took Duke over to buy an overcoat at the
Harvard Coop. Ellington, who must have been close to
sixty at the time, walked in there and they fitted him for
a gabardine overcoat. They went to ring it up, and the
clerk said, "Do you have a student body activity card?"

One night at Storyville, Oscar Marienthal was in the
audience and introduced himself to me after the show,
said he had been asked to see me. He owned Mister
Kelly's in Chicago. It was the same old story. This had
happened to me at the Village Vanguard in New York, and
the hungry i, and was soon to happen at the Interlude in
Hollywood. It was an all-musical room, and they had
never played a comedian. They had their doubts, but they
wondered if I wanted to take a chance. I had to build up

my own network of places to play because the others weren't available to me.

So I went to Chicago and opened up in 1956 with Billie Holiday. Shades of *Lady Sings the Blues*. The movie about Billie, played by Diana Ross, emphasized that white men corrupted her. She was on the road with white men; as I recall, they even had a blond villain in the picture, looming there like a negative, the way they photographed him. I don't recall Billie that way. I recall that the culture base around her was well defined as the drug area, and the participants had done it without our help. But how were we to know that fifteen or seventeen years later the liberals would be going through this self-flagellation? Still, you know the liberals.

The Jewish people have a case of unrequited love for the black man. I remember once when I was on Channel 11 in Los Angeles, which had a different controversial talk show every night, by their own definition—Tom Duggan, Louis Lomax, Joe Pyne, and myself, all of whom are dead except me; how's that for an eerie statistic? Lomax was on one night, and, as an example, he spoke of the disparity between the economic station of Jewish people and black people. He said the black man resents the Jewish store-keeper in the ghetto because he feels that the guy doesn't care about him after he closes his store in Watts and goes back to his home in Beverly Hills. I wonder how many Jewish grocery keepers in Watts have a home in Beverly Hills. Ironically, Louis Lomax had one in the Hollywood Hills. He said to me once at the pool, "This is a wonderful place from which to fight the revolution."

Louis Lomax, who later went into the investigation of the death of Malcolm X, told me he had decided the Central Intelligence Agency had perpetrated the murder and covered it up subsequently. He then went to New Orleans and visited Garrison to discuss the James Earl Ray case

41

and the chief investigator. He denied that he had ever made the original assertions and later died in an auto accident between college lectures. I'm going to refrain from saying anything about the wages of sin, but then again, you might as well have your say, because if you're one inch off their wavelength, they're going to get you anyway.

I guess there are a lot of liberals waiting for me out there in the bushes who are going to say, "Who are they, who are they?" They're not disembodied pronouns. It's a lot like when President Kennedy was killed. How do you look for the motive of that crime? Well, it's not such a conundrum. You just say, "Did the deceased have any enemies?" And you know something, the Warren Commission didn't even ask that question. So, ask it now.

Chicago was really the turning point for me. I settled in there. This was an American city. All the airlines connected there and all the railroads went in and out. And it had its own culture and people weren't afraid to eat steak and corn on the cob and sliced tomatoes. They weren't afraid to be Americans. I picked up a manager again. It's just like changing your socks, only more often. This time it was jazz impresario Norman Granz.

Playboy had decided to do a jazz festival and they were really novices. There's an entertainer in Chicago named Duke Hazlett who's made a life out of imitating Frank Sinatra, both vocally and visually. It's almost a religion. Which Sinatra isn't as faithful to, I might add. Because we were doing the jazz festival in the Chicago Stadium and many people were miles away from the stage, figuratively speaking, Victor Lownes decided to bill a special surprise on the show. And I mean this was a jazz festival that ran for eighteen hours a day. I was the emcee, and I was to say, "Here he is, a real surprise." The rumor had been planted by Lownes that Sinatra would appear. So they sent in the look-alike, with a raincoat and a hat, sur-rounded by policemen to get him to the arena in the mid-dle of this boxing stadium. And the crowd went crazy. And Lownes, being a cynic, of course gloried in it. Then Hazlett came up and sang, and when he was finished, I was supposed to come out and say he was Duke Hazlett, singing at a local club, and give him a plug, which I did. And twenty-two thousand people began to boo me, which was my first lesson in how expensive it is to destroy peo-ple's illusions. Freud said that no one is as disliked as he who decides to shake the sleep of the world.

I found out after that concert that Norman Granz had sold Oscar Peterson and Ella Fitzgerald in there for three songs each for huge sums of money, while I was to emcee all five concerts for practically no money. I was having my trouble with Granz. He was a curious guy. Later, I used to see him in Hollywood at Chasen's, eating alone. He was very bright. He had great taste, al-though somewhat orthodox. He owned a Picasso, and had an office in Beverly Hills, and on his way home he would stop at Ira Gershwin's house and lean on the piano while Fred Astaire sang the lyrics. He liked Frank Sinatra and Ella Fitzgerald as artists. Very orthodox taste. It's sort of like saying, "I always use the teamsters to move my goods."

Granz was argumentative. Anyway, we made five al-bums for Verve Records. One day I was in Granz's office in Beverly Hills soon after we had put out the first comedy record in America. It was called "Mort Sahl, Iconoclast." That shook everybody up because nobody knew what that meant. I brought Shelley Berman and Jonathan Winters to Granz because they both needed to be recorded. Ber-man outsold me. His records sold like magazines, and mine sold more like books. Comedians always compete as if there were one job. Lenny Bruce used to say to me,

"God, I love you, but it's just as if we were in school. One person's going to get an A on the curve, and if there's a choice, I want it to be me, not you."

One problem with Granz was that he lived in Switzerland, so when he left he would leave for thirteen weeks at a time. In his office once, he got into an argument with me about how left I was, versus what he thought I ought to be. And he called me a phony. As he told me this, I was leaving the office, and I pulled the doorknob and it came off in my hand. Here we were, stuck in this office. His secretary called the fire department, who came with an ax to chop a hole in the door to rescue us. And as they came through the door, Norman was recalling the lurid days of his youth. He called after me through the hole in the wall, "If you repeat any of this, I'll deny it." Spoken like a true leftist. Which will explain to a lot of you what happened to the left of America. I can tell you what happened to it recently. Once the government withdrew its financial support, the left had a hard time making its own way on the campus.

The national media became aware of me in 1957. *Playboy* had done its first interview with me in 1956. And *The Reporter*, which was then a great liberal journal, had done an article about me, missing the point, true to the liberal tradition. And then there had been an article in *Holiday* by Alfie Bester. There were others too, and finally, in 1960, *The New Yorker* decided to do a profile about me by Bob Rice, Elmer Rice's son. *Time*, doing a story about me then, rushed their cover because Henry Luce wanted me first. Researching *Time*'s cover story is like performing an FBI security check on a job applicant at the Atomic Energy Commission. They live with you, they record everything, and they keep a file.

Time had me on the cover on August 8, 1960. They called the article within "The Third Campaign." I was on the cover alongside Richard Nixon and John Kennedy. The lead in the article carried a picture of me with Kennedy, because by that time the Democrats had started to ask me to dinners. They weren't as inundated then with spokesmen, believe it or not, as they are today. Now they're blessed with any number of walking encyclopedias: Shirley MacLaine, Warren Beatty, Candice Bergen, and other freethinkers. But at that time, I was it. There I was at the dinners. The dinner featured in the *Time* article was at the Waldorf, for Mrs. Eleanor Roosevelt. It was her seventy-fifth birthday anniversary. We were sitting in a half-moon, starting with John Kennedy, stage right, Harry Belafonte, and myself, going all the way around to Mrs. Roosevelt, Adlai Stevenson, Hubert Humphrey, Thomas K. Finletter, Averell Harriman, and Harry Truman. Truman got up and he said, "This country always starts in the East and works its way West. And tonight it's gonna be different." He had all the presence of Major Bowes, I might add, and sounded like Gene Autry. Truman said, "Tonight we're gonna start in the West and work East. In the interest of Governor Brown of California. When he said that, Kennedy turned to me and said, "Why that old bastard. That means that I'll be the fourteenth speaker." That's exactly what it meant. And that's exactly what he was up to. There was a New York, liberal, Jewish, upper-class crowd in the Waldorf that night. Kennedy was planning on making some friends among the liberal elite, who were very much in love with Adlai Stevenson, and if not him, the next best girl in town, Hubert Humphrey. Jack turned to me and said, "Goddam it, what a curse." I said, "Well, you just might survive it." Those people really had conviction. They didn't cheer until it looked like he might get the nomination; then they genuflected.

Which Jack knew even then. The crowd had a broker's sensitivity.

Belafonte at that time was a good friend of Brando's, and they were both active in the civil rights marches and so on. And one day I was walking in Hollywood when I was out of work and I ran into Belafonte going to rehearsal at the Rainbow Studios. And he grunted at me and asked me if I was working anywhere, where I was making waves these days. And I said, "Have you seen Marlon?" He said, "I don't talk to him." I got to thinking about *The Defiant Ones,* with Tony Curtis and Sidney Poitier. The Curtis part was offered to one actor, who said he wouldn't work with a Negro, and it was offered to Kirk Douglas, who wanted to play the Negro, and then it was offered to Brando, who wanted to play both roles.

So I said to Belafonte, "You don't talk to Marlon?" And he said, "At a point in the upward struggle of my people he was there to be used and we used him." And I looked at this guy. He's a latter-day folk singer who used to sit at the Royal Roost in 1948 in New York with a Billy Eckstein collar and a Windsor knot, trying to be a jazz singer. But it catches up with everybody. Where are they now? Occasionally Belafonte can be seen emceeing *The Tonight Show.* He usually has a guest like Ted Kennedy. Talks to him about everything except—you know—about salami and dirigibles, but never mentions his brothers.

While I was at Mister Kelly's once, Shecky Greene, who was a local boy who made good, was supporting Ann Sothern at the Chez Paree. There are clubs that people associate with ownership by gangsters, as in the movies. Actually, gangsters are extremely stable in their investments and would never dream of subsidizing a nightclub. I wanted to see Shecky one night, and in the lounge of the Chez Paree was a radio show; that was the custom in those days—broadcast journalism, I think they called it.

Jack Eigen was the broadcaster. He'd sit there with a buxom blonde who would take phone calls. Example: "Jack, a listener wants to know what you think of Joseph Stalin." Jack would say, "Joseph Stalin knows what I think of him." You see, this guy was pretty influential for a Chicago broadcaster.

So I walked in and he said, "I heard about you. You're a professional nonconformist who wears a sweater. How far do you think you'll get in our business that way?" So I said, "Well, I really like to feel comfortable when I'm working." And he said, "Well, you're going to alienate people if you keep this up. You're not Marlon Brando. You can't afford to be a nonconformist. You won't have any friends." So I said, "Well, as Einstein said, I'll have to live in that solitude which is painful in adolescence, but delicious in maturity." And Eigen said, "Yeah. Well, Sophie Tucker said life is nothing without friends." So I said, "Jack, we've each appealed to a higher authority, now we'll have to wait for a verdict."

Lenny Bruce was then working at the Gate of Horn in back of Kelly's. It was owned by Al Grossman, who said he was a man of the people. We all used to go help the club out because it was bankrupt. Later, when he managed Bob Dylan, he found a way to put the people on hold.

Is there anything in America that's as sour as former leftists? What the hell happened to those guys? I suppose that's what's wrong with communism in America. The cadre here, instead of being farmers and students, as in Cuba, was the Screen Writers Guild. The average communist in America made $150,000 per picture. But they sure did disappear. Budd Schulberg lived long enough to turn some of them in and then go down to Watts and organize a group of angry, carping, illiterate Negroes and call them writers.

47

Chicago had another thing. It had four newspapers, and it had Colonel McCormick running the *Tribune*. I used to get a big laugh when I'd look at the *Tribune* and say, "Well, it looks like war . . . with England." It had mostly Irv Kupcinet. And Kup, of course, was the compendium of the old-time columnists and still is. Kup was a champion of mine until he thought I lost my way. He had a television show, and very few of the celebrities who came through Chicago weren't available to him, so he could really put the names on. I did the show many dozens of times. It was a talk show, and it used to be open-ended, going three or four hours into the early morning Sunday. Started Saturday night, after the movie, of course. It was a talk show with interesting kinds of people on it. They'd have a Republican black lawyer who had made something of himself—I think that was the way they put it. And sometimes they would have a black revolutionary or student from SDS who was plugging a book. And a movie star whose jewels had been stolen from her hotel while she was taping the show. And somebody who was doing a bad play somewhere in the suburbs.

While I was in Chicago the manager of the Drury Lane Theatre once said to me, "Our audience is full of hicks. They don't want to see good theater; they just want to see television stars, and I'm going to book accordingly." And after that, I think he presented *Beckett* with Howard K. Smith or Harry Reasoner, and *Tea and Sympathy* with Merv Griffin and Virginia Graham. I don't want to tempt you anymore theatrically. It's back to literature.

I used to do a routine: One night Kup had LeRoi Jones on the air, and I think it was really the synthesis of everything that's wrong with talk shows on the air. Here's this guy sitting there, the liberal sitting on the panel, saying, "What is it that you want, Sir?" And, of course, Jones is saying something to the effect of "Your head." And he's angry, and they're intimidated, and at one point he says, "We're gong to burn society to the ground." Then Kup says, "Well, we have to stop for a commercial." When they come back, they get on another subject, and LeRoi Jones turns around and says, "What happened? We were going to burn everything to the ground."

When you're a revolutionary, you can't put your torch in the umbrella stand while they do a commercial. That's what they don't understand in America. Don't get me wrong. I appreciate what we've done in this country. In fact, I'm glad we have a working model.

Once, when Chet Huntley went on vacation at NBC in 1957, John Chancellor got in touch with me and said he was going to do a show while Huntley was out of the country. Chancellor came out to my house on the beach at Malibu and there were hundreds of people coming in —there always are when you live on the beach at Malibu. So he came out there with an NBC film crew and he filmed me and he said, "You're the most gregarious man I know. What are your opinions?" And I told him about the H-bomb and what Bertrand Russell had said in warning us about the H-bomb, something to the effect that, if memory serves me, we would have mutations if we kept experimenting with these bombs in the atmosphere. About that time some kid came along collecting money for the Boy Scouts and he was a member of the Mickey Mouse Club and he had one of those hats with Mickey Mouse ears. Here's this kid with these ears and I decided the tests had gone far enough.

Chancellor then showed, the same evening that my interview went on, the least gregarious man he knew, a hermit living in a packing crate in a hobo jungle outside of Omaha. And he asked him his opinions of America, since he'd been away from American society for twenty or thirty years. He asked him about the H-bomb. And the guy said the same thing I did. Makes you think, doesn't it?

Chet Huntley later told me that the worst thing about working with me was that he couldn't edit me. He said, "You go on in this endless cadence and there are no seams along which to cut." I always had a kinship with the newsmen because news people like Chancellor and Art Buchwald and, later, Dan Rather, any number of them, come to laugh. Especially during the innocent days when the Democrats were really rebels. Not the young against the old, or black against white, or male against female. What happened in the '60's was that the adversaries got larger. It got so that the women's movement called women the "niggers" of our time and confused gender with class.

Newsmen always gave me the stories they couldn't use anywhere else. They worked in a collective effort, and I was in a reasonably free form that spoiled me. It's a great luxury to get up and say what you think. Although Freud cautioned us, "It's easier to say what you think than to know what you think."

Throughout all that period and all this, for that matter, I found that humor makes the tragedy of living bearable. When you attack humanity, you are granted a certain immunity. This axiom about the broadness of the attack and its immunity is not a harmless generalization. Later, in the '60's, we saw the pernicious effect of accepting the big crimes—the assassinations, the war—and classifying the small crimes as violations of law and order.

Jane Dick had told Adlai Stevenson about me and he became a frequent visitor at Mister Kelly's. He used to come in with his law partner and eventual campaign manager, William McCormick Blair, a patrician of sorts, or maybe just a Middle Western Ivy Leaguer. Stevenson would walk into the club and people would grab him and say, "I voted for you, Governor," and he would say, "Yes, I met the other one recently too."

Of course, he had favorite jokes. He loved it when I talked about the time when Dulles hired him to write speeches about Eisenhower at the State Department, how they never invited him along and his feelings were hurt. So he would wave his fist out the door as he saw the black limousines going to the Burning Tree golf club for lunch and yell, "Big Business." Well, he loved that, and one night he came into the club with Hubert Humphrey, and we went to the men's room together and Humphrey said to me in the men's room, "I'm worried about how we are going to negotiate with the Russians, because they're smarter than Dulles." At that time I was doing jokes about Dulles, like "He flies now and we pay later." He said they're smarter than we are, but they're also unscrupulous —lack of ethics plus cunning; how do you beat that combination? He always had those concerns, Humphrey.

Stevenson invited me up to his farm in Libertyville. I used to drive up there on weekends or my night off. He had a great rambling den in the basement and the walls were covered with the original drawings of all the political cartoonists who had attacked him, and, believe me, they were legion. That was when this country had what were known as Republican newspapers. He showed me where he used to write his speeches in longhand. He showed me very proudly the twenty-four blackface Suffolk sheep that Winston Churchill had given him.

I came out after dinner one night to go home and there was a reporter waiting for me in the bushes from *Time* magazine and he said, "What were you and Governor Stevenson discussing?" Stevenson said we were discussing the fact that a sheepskin was a handicap in American politics. Stevenson was so honorable that, of all the people I've known who've run for office, he never once asked for anything but my company. He never asked me whether I endorsed him, whether I would work for him. In the later years, when he worked for Jack Kennedy, I would meet him at many of the rallies, and, in fact, I appeared at a lot of them largely for him, because I never worked for the Kennedy candidacy. I never worked for anybody's. But I believe that you should take politics into the theater. I'm not so sure that you should take theater into politics. I have a unique advantage.

We were having dinner one Sunday at Stevenson's ranch—roast beef and corn on the cob. He was from Illinois all right. But even so, he never understood a lot of politics because he couldn't countenance the things that were beneath him. Not like Harry Truman, of whom liberals are constantly saying, "I was wrong. I'm re-evaluating him." Liberals can't re-evaluate Bertrand Russell; they're busy with Harry Truman, the feisty bantam rooster, clothing salesman, and Pendergast candidate, and perpetrator of the Cold War, and as much a betrayer of Franklin D. Roosevelt with Leahy at his elbow as Lyndon Johnson was of John Kennedy.

Adlai Stevenson was the only candidate I ever met who knew, if he was ever elected, the first guy to attack him would be me. He expected it and he didn't resent it. The only time we ever argued was about Fidel Castro. He couldn't understand why I was thrilled by the revolution. He said, "Don't you think that in the final analysis this Castro fellow is quite unstable?" I said, "He shows no evidence of it, but I thought we did in fire-bombing him. The CIA going in there every night without filing a flight plan, bombing the sugar-cane fields."

I don't know if anyone here in America really understands revolution anyway. I'm not talking about the agents provocateurs we would see in later years who infiltrated the left and tried to make it into a heinous cartoon to try to turn off young people from joining it. I'm talking about the guys who give their lives, who say, "I know I can die doing this, but let's get on with it." I don't think Americans can encompass that, anybody who believes in anything to that degree. It's just alien to us, and we can't deal with it because of that. Our leftists are not really dangerous, not because they're not extremists, but because they don't believe in anything. Not that much. In black or white. After all, did anyone organize a Lincoln Brigade for Chile?

Stevenson was intuitive about how I feel about liberals. He once said to me, "You approve of me, don't you?" And I said, "Yes, Governor, I do." And he said, "Can't you find any flaws?" So I laughed and said, "No, sir." And he said, "Well, it's obvious. What's the worst thing about me?" He said, "It's apparent." And I said, "What?" and he said, "The worst thing about me is my supporters."

My biggest battle up to that point was not political. It was people in the business who staved me off. The agents, all in all, were hoping I'd go away. I was booking myself. Was I a bona fide success? Well, I showed all the signs—but as Charlton Heston pointed out, you're not a success until you've been sued. Well, I was closer to that than I knew. Like the Treasure of the Sierra Madre, I was standing right on top of the site.

I found a manager. His name was Frank Nichols. This fellow was eminently qualified to manage me. He had produced a religious series on Sunday. You know, the kind that has a lesson at eight o'clock in the morning. It was called *Look Up and Live*. At that time the Church was in love with Dave Brubeck, using him on their shows. Through Brubeck I met Nichols, and Nichols became my manager. He decided that I should work in New York, and so I went back to the Village Vanguard—the scene of my earlier triumphs. I had worked at the Blue Angel in New York and I had been there with Jonathan Winters when we were both breaking in. The Blue Angel was owned by Herbert Jacoby and Max Gordon, but Jacoby owned the Vanguard alone. Gordon was another disappointed freethinker who kept saying to me, "The times have changed. It used to be that a guy like you would be appreciated politically, but these people don't come out, and they don't want to change the world."

The Village Vanguard in New York is next to a subway, and I can tell you from experience that they do run on time. The supporting act when I opened at the Vanguard was Mike Nichols and Elaine May. And I was astonished that she had made a name playing a Jewish girl from the Bronx. I mean, the audience was loaded with Jewish boys who spent their lives running away from her, and here they were standing in line to hear the utterances. And I couldn't believe they thought they were funny. Mike Nichols at that time fancied himself a radical and contributed to all good causes by checkbook. He changed a lot when he emerged and became a traffic cop in Doc Simon comedies on Broadway, and when he utilized repressed sexuality in the movies. His ultimate triumph is a movie called *Carnal Knowledge*. In it two men go from puberty to maturity; they grow up in America, discussing sex. They never once mention the stock market or Joe McCarthy. You've encountered such men, maybe. In my experience I never found anyone with that kind of staying power. Nichols tried current events with *Day of the Dolphin*, which the CIA could have written, in which right-wing maniacs want to kill the President, and when a CIA agent is asked if his illegal activities are sanctioned by the government he answers, "Which one? There are several governments." To protect and to serve became to confuse and deplete.

New York went very well because I said everything they wanted to say and thought they should say. I give Elaine May credit. I remember her saying something to the effect that he's probably the most commercial of all the comedians because people like to think they understand him and they make every effort. The New York comedians talked about their mothers-in-law and continually said to me, "How can you live in a cultural desert, California?" I still didn't really live anywhere. The index is that I've always owned portable radios. They didn't even plug in. So all these actors, people that I knew, would go back and forth. They'd go to Hollywood to make a picture and then they'd go back. I might add that the reverence that actors like Paul Newman had for New York was shared by all of them, and as a result they went to Hollywood to drink from the trough and run. And Hollywood showed the ravished effects of people who came only to take. I think it still does residually. It's a tapped area.

I just worked, and I fed on it. I wrote a show for the Bijou Theater on 45th Street called *The Next President,* which opened in 1958. I had a Greek chorus. The entertainment was made up of some people you know: Mary Travers, of Peter, Paul, and Mary, and the folk singer Eric Darling. I hired another of Nichols' acts—here we go again with nepotism—Jimmy Giuffre, a jazz group that did a sort of compendium swamp music in jazz, what they used to call folk funk.

That was one of the several times I invested in jazz. I created a stereo orchestra: two separate units, and the band was scored for A section and B section, and it was rehearsed that way. I remember one day one of the trombone players said, "Bill, when the guys in the other band are playing Letter A . . ." And a little later on, I subsidized a Kenton alumnus, Dee Barton. He had two bands in one, six men on one side and twenty-nine men on the other. He used to caution them, "I'll dial you in electronically. You'll never know what the other band is gonna play. Only I have command." Don Menza, the saxophone player, said, "Is it all right if we fraternize with the guys in the other band at the bar?"

I may be the only entertainer who's ever become an honorary musician. I won the Entertainer of the Year award from *Metronome Magazine* for three years in a row, the only nonmusician so named. I was valedictorian of the Newport Jazz Festival. And I emceed the first Monterey Jazz Festival. I found a great kinship with musicians because I found they're like athletes. Their talent is pure. It cannot be challenged. It's prime. We shared humor and unbridled imagination and optimism. Some funny things happen around musicians. I also worked Lenny's, on the turnpike in Boston, theretofore strictly a jazz club. When Kenton worked it he brought in twenty-five guys, and Lenny Sokolov, the proprietor, said, "It's gonna be a thrill to have Stan here." And I said, "How do you get twenty-five entertainers into a club that seats only one hundred customers?" Lenny answered, "Well, we have to take some tables out." And I said, "Well, how can you make any money?" And he said, "Because none of my customers drinks as much as Stan Kenton and his orchestra."

One night when I was working at Donte's, Stan came in and said, "I'd like to make an album of just band stories, a vocal album, that is, a talking album, called 'Private Party.' We'll invite all the alumni of the band and get them to talk, and I'll close the room and serve them booze, and you and I will emcee, encouraging the people to talk." We were in a room for eight hours one night—from nine until five in the morning. And talk they did.

For example, the story was told of how Chet Baker, the trumpet player in exile in Italy, once played a jam session after the war with Romeo Mussolini, the dictator's son, and he didn't know how to approach Mussolini. So he walked up on the stage, leaned over on the piano, and said, "Sorry to hear about your dad."

And Med Florey, an actor who used to be in the Thornhill band and now leads a group called "Super Sax," which re-creates Charlie Parker's great solos in a unison section, told how he went on the road with a band. The band didn't have a bus; it had five cars. Men of the same affinity, of course, rode in the same cars. It's just like men rooming together in college. And there were four clean cars and one junkie car. Florey was a young kid just starting out and the junkies were otherwise occupied, so they let him drive. They had a lot of "hit and run" jobs, as the musicians called them in those days, which meant that they would close one day in, say, Orlando, Florida, and have to open up the next night in Vancouver—so they'd drive like hell all night. When Florey couldn't stay awake, the junkies gave him a pill; and when he couldn't sleep, the junkies gave him a pill. Pretty soon his head began to drum, and he found himself at a service station lying in the middle of a road. So the junkies got out of the car and threw a glass of water on his face and slipped him back behind the wheel. He said, "What are you doing?" And they said, "Well, we took a vote and we decided you're in the best physical condition of anybody in the car, so you should drive." At the end of the tour, the other four cars had twenty-six thousand miles on them, and the junkie car had forty-one thousand miles on it because the guys were always taking off after a job to drive a hundred miles to meet a nurse, front man, or other connection.

Back to Broadway. I opened. Ignorance, my God, is bliss. I broke every theatrical convention by sitting on the apron and talking to the audience without preparing material. Sold out every night. And got reasonably good reviews. Next door to the Bijou, at the Morosco, Richard Burton was appearing with Helen Hayes and Susan Strasberg in *Time Remembered*. He used to come over when he was changing costume, to stand in the wings and watch my show, because he said I changed my show every night. We got to be fast friends.

Famous people are really open. They're lonely. While I was there, in New York, I was staying at the Algonquin. Some of the other people staying at the hotel were Laurence Olivier, who was doing *The Entertainer;* and playwright John Osborne, who had another play on Broadway, *Look Back in Anger*, starring the late Mary Ure, then his wife.

The night I opened my show, Mary Ure said to me, "You have to rest all day; you can't get out of bed." And she came into my suite at the Algonquin and made me dinner in the hotel room. She sent me flowers. "Men never get flowers, and women should think of it more often. You like them, don't you?"

Later I saw Mary and John in California. The first time they came to my house in California I had an overnight guest. We panicked: the guest ran upstairs and I ran downstairs. Mary and John, meanwhile, made ham and eggs for four. There was only one door out of the house, so when the young lady came downstairs—she was blushing—Mary said simply, "Sit down and have some ham and eggs." I said, "Listen, I'm going to be frank. I didn't know you were coming over, and I thought you might be kind of surprised if you found out there were two of us here." And Mary said, "We'd only be surprised if there weren't two of you here." It's not so hard growing up with friends like that.

Closing notices went up for the show thirteen days after it opened. There was no lack of audience, but there was a lack of funds for operating capital. The audience was there, but the show was closing. There was no accounting for it.

I went back to California, to the Crescendo in Hollywood. I went for four weeks and I stayed for eighty-eight. In my case the reason was, "If you can't stop him, absorb him." How did they do that? Well, I met starlets. I was always meeting starlets. These girls would sit in the car and say, "I want to be an actress." And I would say, "Why?" And they would say, "Because I have something to say." "What do you have to say?" I would ask. "I want to be an actress." Sorry, panel, we don't have enough time to go around again. I suppose in this era young girls you pick up hitchhiking on the Strip would not say, "I want to be an actress." Nowadays, they would more likely say, "I want to direct."

I made the mistake early in my career, when I moved to Hollywood, of being attracted to actresses. I used to go out exclusively with actresses and all other female impersonators. First of all, let's get sex out of the way. It's kind of like a date. Let's get that out of the way first, and then we can talk. First of all, if you can talk after sex, you really have something big going. Sex is impersonal. The con job done on young guys in this culture is amazing, convincing them of this great gift that women can give you. Actually, it's the least they can give you. If people don't want you to get personal, they get you on a physical basis and that keeps you at arm's length.

The fact is that you can't have a good relationship

with a girl who hasn't settled things with her father. All girls answer as follows: "Well, what about guys who don't settle things with their mothers?" That's not as crucial to me, because I'm not looking for a guy. The thing is that women, if they could look at their fathers objectively, and make an estimate of them, and see where they failed, and forgive them and forget them, they'd be all right. Because they haven't settled things with them, men become the road company of their fathers. "*He* never paid any attention to me, either." You've got nothing but trouble. The thing about women is that they don't discriminate. Even though they hate you and they think you're insensitive, they won't let on, and they'll marry you and punish you.

Women also have a great weakness that we don't have. You know, they keep saying in the Movement that they're the same as we are. But they're *not* the same. For instance, I don't think that women think about honor as anything but a weakness. Women are not romantics and have no mercy. When a woman is cold, she'll cancel you out of the human race. A nurse from the third floor of a hospital, when you call to ask about a patient who is in Intensive Care, is more personal and will give you more of her time than a woman who has lived with you for five years and decided she doesn't want to anymore so that she can be fulfilled.

Fulfillment for a woman is like graduating in psychiatric social work. Fulfillment for a woman is to test. Steve Allen and the people, the Committee for Nuclear Policy, would say, "For God's sake, stop the testing." Women are always testing. They want to see how far they can go. Do you know when they're fulfilled? When you tell them not to go any further or you'll brain them. That's when they really think they've found a safe harbor. It's sad that it has to be that primitive. But in a woman's eyes a man's sensitivity will never be valued the way his strength is.

Everybody in L.A. thought I was from San Francisco. And I went along with the myth, but I finally had come home again. Only, L.A. was different. I wasn't living in South Gate, I was living in Hollywood. And everybody I used to see in the movies was coming to see the show. In Hollywood I went to parties. I was in Hollywood people's movies, and I was in their television shows, but I didn't go to their Democratic Party rallies. The question was, would I stay? I didn't, of course. I knew what the touch of their embrace was, and then I began to know what their fist felt like.

Gene Norman, who was a disc jockey in Los Angeles, owned the Crescendo in Hollywood. Norman paid for everything in cash. He didn't have *two* sets of books—he didn't even have *one*. He had a young woman named Robin that he went around with who kept his books, and he trusted her, which was a level some guys never reach with a woman. And he'd been a boy genius—gone to the University of Michigan and Berkeley and gradually got a Ph.D. in philosophy at sixteen, so he had a license to be unhappy. The first night I opened, he took me to a drive-in in Los Angeles for breakfast. They don't have carhops there, they have a radio speaker into which you call your order. And he, of course, had been a disc jockey all his life, so when the speaker barked in his ear and said, "Order, please," he cleared his throat, cupped his hand to his ear, and said, "Good evening, two cheeseburgers, please." He used to have a marquee over his club that said, "Gene Norman Presents Jazz," which we changed one night to say, "Gene Norman *Prevents* Jazz."

I worked in the Interlude upstairs. Downstairs, Jerry Sothern had the commercial acts like the Mary Kaye Trio. And a house comedian named Lenny Bruce. And Lenny Bruce used to sit there and play sophomoric antiauthoritarian games. One night through the ventilator I heard him playing a prom—we had three or four hundred high school kids—and he had them chanting "Lynch Mort Sahl." Then he'd come upstairs to my club and order a drink and then say very loudly, "Let's see, ten cents for the cost of liquor, five cents for labor." He'd itemize the bill and then start to yell, "You are crooks, you are crooks." If he could make people uncomfortable, he enjoyed it. In fact, his view was that if he could make an audience uncomfortable, they had taken the first first step toward understanding. Of course, that's not true. You can't extort communication.

I used to go down and catch his show and he would come up and catch my show. This was before the liberals got hold of him. And the Civil Liberties attorneys. At that time he didn't swear, he just talked about the movies. And he was pretty damn funny. Ad-libbed a lot, which very few do even today. His ad lib being you can say anything you want.

One night a guy came in to see Lenny and said he was Shelley Berman's nephew. And Lenny pretended to be all impressed and said, "Yeah, I heard all about you." And the kid said, "Yeah? I work a lot like you and Mort. I tell what happened to me all day. I just sort of wing it." Lenny said, "That's good, that's what we do." Then he went out on the stage and said, "I have a great surprise for you folks. We have a great comedian here tonight, Howie Berman." And the kid said, "I can't get up there." And Lenny said, "Sure you can." Kid said, "What'll I do?" Lenny said, "Tell 'em what you did all day." So the kid got on stage and we all cringed for half an hour while the kid told about going to the dry cleaner's and getting his car washed and getting change for the telephone. And Lenny just sat there ecstatically watching this guy drown. Sort of high gallows humor. I found Lenny to be a funny comedian, a great impersonator, and a very sentimental guy. I did not find him profound, and I disagree with those who now put him on the cross. Even Lenny knew that only *you* can kill yourself.

I was working one night and a girl with great cheek-bones came up to me after the show. She said, "That was fantastic." It was Phyllis Kirk. Phyllis and I began to go out. She wanted to be an actress because she had something to say, which she managed not to do the whole time I knew her. Eventually she said, "Well, we're going to get married." It was her decision. Marlene Dietrich once told me about relationships with actresses. "It's like having two jobs," she said. "You've got a job. What do you need her as a job for?" I asked her what she meant. She said, "If she doesn't have a job, she'll drive you crazy. And if she has a job, you'll never see her."

Anyway, Phyllis said to me at one point, "Well, we're going to get married, and I want to get our lives organized, so I'm doing this television series, *The Thin Man*, with Peter Lawford." (Those of you who saw Howard Hughes's wonderful film *The Outlaw* may remember Peter Lawford, the star of *The In-Law*.) Sinatra called Lawford America's guest; he went from Frank Sinatra's back to Jack Kennedy's back. (I said to Kennedy, "What are you going to do when you leave office?" Jack replied, "That's not the question. What's Peter going to do?") Last time I saw him he was on Sammy Davis's back, which is sort of like a full-grown man riding a mule. So, Lawford and Phyllis were doing a show at MGM, and I went out there and met Sinatra, who was on the next stage doing *Some Came Running*. I met Lawford's manager, Milton Ebbins, who had been a band boy for Count Basie, and manager for Billy Eckstein. Phyllis wanted me to sign with him. I did, and also with her agency, the William Morris Agency, signing with Sam Weisbord. Here, I'd like to give everybody's credentials. I think Lenny Bruce referred to Sam Weisbord as a dwarf. Myself, I didn't see any signs of it.

When I reflect on my life with women, I recall that Paul Newman said to me, "You always give lugubrious, heavy gifts. Because you can't relate to people in a tender way." Newman and the others, they're all psychologists. You know, I always used to travel the college concerts and I carried my own airline guides so I'd know how in hell to get out of these godforsaken towns like Disappear, New Mexico. Warren Beatty said to me, "That shows your parents abandoned you and you're always insecure 'cause you don't know quite where you are." It's what Herb Shriner used to call free advice, and it's worth every cent of it. Well, it was just that I needed some kind of contact, to take someone's hand and have them press it back. Bill Dana used to kid me about that. I gave him a watch. And he used to walk up onstage and say, "Mort Sahl gave me this watch. You press this button and it presses back and makes you feel wanted." That was before sensitivity training came in. What's everybody training for anyway? Don't touch me, I'm in training.

Beatty used to go to Dr. Martin Grotjahn in Beverly Hills, who wrote a book called *Jewish Wit*, which is not my biography, by the way. The book is an analysis of Jewish humor and shows great wonderment at how prolific the Jewish people are. Of course Grotjahn is Viennese, but he's not Jewish. He's Gentile, and he must be, because I don't know of anybody who would be so overwhelmed by the Jewish people as to characterize them as supernatural. Unfortunately, the Jewish people are all too human, which makes them stop just short of the greatness that is promised many times in their performance and seldom realized. When the chips are down, they react like everybody else. Dubious ambition. At least that's what they used to say about the blacks and others are saying about women. What do you want? I want to be like you. I wouldn't help anybody who wanted to be like me. They'll have to transcend me to make it a worthy ambition.

As for Phyllis, I wandered over to her house between shows at the Crescendo one night about 11:30 to give her the emerald ring and ask her to marry me. And she was watching television, eating chocolates, buffing her nails. Probably taking a correspondence course in telepathy at the same time. Anyway, I said, haltingly, "I've been married. I never thought I'd do it twice. But this thing had come up. I really thought we could help each other through the mortal storm." And I was fumbling, admittedly, for the words. She turned to me in an unguarded moment, when she didn't have her eyes lined and wasn't at the studio, and said, "What the fuck are you talking about?" It was like a lash across my back. I don't like profanity anyway. You haven't read any here. I'm sorry you had to read that. In addition to reducing us all to a graphic crudity, cursing sets up arbitrary active and passive roles, so that all that distinguishes male from female is only what distinguishes victim from victimizer.

Phyllis was fond of revisiting all the people who've given her a prognosis of doom in her career. Which I suppose is redundant, because she equated that with her life. Her career might be said to be smaller than life. But she'd been that way since the first time she'd done a walk-on in Leland Hayward's *Point of No Return* in New York and been fired immediately. She wanted to go back with me to show everybody she had risen from the ashes.

I'd find myself in social situations inside these various alabaster palaces, shrines that people who contributed nothing to society insist on building to themselves. And the conversation ran the same way. The women who now talk about tennis then talked about the weather, the texture of fabrics, and called such things either "heaven" or "divine," which, of course, is a town in the same precinct. The men did the same thing as they do now. They talked about money. See, men are really aliens on the planet. Women think if worst comes to worst, I can revalidate my credentials if I can have a child. Because they're in direct succession with life. Men are basically aliens. They have to prove their merit; there has to be a reason for their being on staff.

Women now call it the Liberation Movement, and I'm sure that that appeals to an awful lot of people. Because whenever you go on television as a guest, you can say, "Here's a leader of the Women's Movement." It's like the Black Movement used to be. It didn't have any followers. It just had leaders. And that in itself is appealing. Still, I've noticed that women come off best when in the company of men, as Bertrand Russell pointed out. Outstanding women, it seems to me, like Barbara Tuchman and Lillian Hellman, never emphasize their gender. They just happen to be good writers. That is beyond gender. Gloria Steinem is always telling us what the housewife in Montana might be, given the opportunity. And it's gratuitous because there never is full liberation, and we'll never know, and the burden is upon us.

I broke up with Phyllis in 1960. She had asked me to introduce her to Jack Kennedy. I did. The next day she showed up at his suite at the Beverly Hills Hotel without me. Of course, since Kennedy met so many people, he worked on a system of associations. As soon as she walked in, he said, "How's Mort?" She said, "How would I know? I'm not his keeper. I'm a person too." So he threw his hands up and wouldn't talk to her.

Finally I asked her to take a trip with me. I said I was going to stop all activity and take a vacation. I said one couldn't really know another person until they had trav-

eled together. She said all right. Then, as the week of
traveling got closer and closer, she got very nervous. So
I asked her to have lunch. I went to lunch to tell her I
was letting her off the hook, that the trip was merely a
test anyway. I said, "I don't think I want to take you on
this trip." So she said, "Well, I called you to tell you I
can't go because I've met somebody. And I'm in love."
That was between a Wednesday and a Friday. That's the
great thing about being promiscuous: there can't be too
much wrong with someone who believes in love. She said,
"I've met this wonderful man." I knew him. He was a
homosexual. But that was all right. She was a great nurse,
provided you had a great problem—like being a homosexual or losing your television series.

I used to go out with a girl named Tippie Hedren,
whom Hitchcock discovered. One day he gave a cast party
for her when she was making the movie *The Birds*, and
I was driving her up to the Beverly Wilshire to attend it.
She said, "Please don't come in. Hitch doesn't like you.
He says if I hang around with you, you'll ruin things.
There's no reason why we have to break up. He just can't
see you. He's somewhat possessive." So I said, "What do
you mean I'll ruin your life?" "Hitch said you ruined
Phyllis Kirk's life. And you ruined Shirley MacLaine's life."
I stopped the car in the middle of traffic and threw her
out. I said, "Don't be late for the party!" She said, "Mort,
I'm an actress. And that's as dedicated a profession as a
doctor's. You've got to understand that." Trying to grasp
the analogy, I said, "I don't follow you. If I don't go to see
one of your movies, I won't die." I drove away. I wonder
what it is about all these beautiful girls—that is, when you
walk away from them, let alone break up with them, you
feel like you just got out of Folsom Prison.

At the Crescendo, and later on, I watched the fever
come to the Strip as only it can with an audience when

you crystallize what's been on their minds. And in 1957 I was laying out for them everything they wanted to say about Eisenhower. The President was out to lunch. And it's easy to laugh at a guy like that. I mean, he wasn't vicious, so they didn't have to worry about rebelling against the king and getting hurt. Something quite different would happen later in my life when I kidded about the Warren Commission. As long as it was a clerical error, and not a heinous conspiracy, people could deal with it. They could laugh at bunglers because nothing has to be done about them. It's really a case of bureaucratic inefficiency. It would be easier if it were. I wish it were and I could have told everybody. It would have been a lot easier on me.

I used to stand out in front of the club and read magazines in the summer. And a guy who looked like he just came from the gym came up to me and said, "Mr. Sahl, rarely have I heard a compendium of subjects so adequately covered as you did tonight." He invited me to dinner the next night. Joanne Woodward was the first one to come to dinner; Newman was late. He was at Warner Brothers making a movie called *The Silver Chalice*, which you may have seen on "The Late Show," in which Virginia Mayo in a memorable scene visits him in a compound in Rome where he's in chains and she says, "Why, Basil, you're a slave." It was shot either in a slave compound in Rome or in the commissary while Newman was under a term contract. And I got there early and talked with Joanne and she was terribly shy. She considered herself an ugly duckling and she had gone through psychoanalysis, the Neighborhood Playhouse, and the ultimate trauma— which is not acting, of course, that's shelter—the trauma of meeting a married man. During *Picnic* she met Newman and kept telling him to leave his wife and he wouldn't. Finally, one day, he did and showed up on her doorstep with a suitcase and she really panicked. Then she had the same problem his wife had—why does this happen to me? None of us is safe.

All of my friends looked upon me as lost. Newman was forever having me over for dinner and on Sunday afternoons at the pool, saying, "Well, Mort's all alone." He used to drink and talk a lot. He'd start in the afternoon hoisting daiquiris on the lawn and go through Bloody Marys and beer with dinner and brandy and stingers afterward. He used to take a large brandy snifter and fill it with ice cubes and brandy and Scotch and sit in the lotus position in the sauna. He asked me to go in there with him and I did. He once cried over a negative review of a film which his mother mailed him. This was while Newman is making a million and a half dollars per picture. Newman, by the way, was fond of saying things like "I want to change the world, but I have to eat." He was working a lot because Brando didn't want to work. And he was Brando's road company—at least physically. He wasn't nearly as interesting.

Joanne had an apartment in New York on 55th Street and First Avenue, and when I went back to work a night club in New York or do a television show, Newman would insist that I use the apartment while they were in California, which I did. One time when I was in the apartment, Newman called me and told me that Ed Murrow was going to do *Person to Person* with "Jobo," as he called Joanne. And he said, "You gotta hurry up and get my clothes out of the apartment, because the CBS crew is coming over to stage the show." That was one of the more hectic days. Which shows you how things have changed. Today you say, "We live together and we're not going to get married," and people say, "Well, you have no right to do that unless the girl's pregnant." Or, "Why are you living with a girl?" It's not a permissive era. It's no more permissive than Los Angeles is casual. It's indifferent. It refuses to be offended.

Newman then was on the cover of Hefner's new publication, *Show Business Illustrated*. It was Hefner's Vietnam. They called Newman the new brand of screen lover and inside it said, "Newman, when pressed, names comedian Mort Sahl as his best friend." They made it sound like the Red Chinese had used the water torture or thumb screws and he finally revealed my name along with his name, rank, and serial number. All this time Newman used to say to me in the steam bath, "Why do you have to make a million and why do you have to be famous?" He was now grossing about five million a year. He said, "You're special. You're to be treasured. You should just speak one or two times a year to the liberals who understand you." That's the one thing, boy. I'm like a natural resource; people want to conserve me.

Once I was working at the Cafe Au Go Go in New York. I had to keep going back to the scenes of my crimes as Newman kept ascending. I mean, I was going back to work in Greenwich Village in my sweater, because, after all, "Mort, you want to talk to your people, don't you?" (I have the luxury of talking to my people and of subsidizing them as well. Let me tell you, Negroes, that nobody has been conspired against as much as the American people. Spat upon, reviled, milked, cajoled, exploited, taxed, exhumed from the dead—when they weren't merely written off as dead. It's partially their own fault. They don't scream enough in their anguish.)

Well, Newman was now living in Westport; he'd bought a carriage house in Connecticut. And he drove a Volkswagen because he didn't want to be pretentious in case anybody was looking. And he used to get through with his show at eleven and come over and pick me up after my late show at one o'clock and drive me to Westport. I lived with him, which was his idea. For a guy who didn't even live with his parents all his life, here I was with my surrogate folks. So he came down one night to the Cafe Au Go Go and brought with him Elizabeth Taylor and Richard Burton—Burton at that time was playing *Hamlet*. So they came to the club, and the word had gotten out that they were going to be there, and Les Crane was there with ABC cameras; he was a controversial late-night host at that time. So, they all walked into the Cafe Au Go Go and it was like Christmas at Macy's. Everybody wanted to see Elizabeth Taylor and Paul Newman. And they all swamped over the stage and finally into my dressing room. A guy from the New York *Post* said to Burton, "What are you doing here?" Burton said, "Well, I always come to see Mort." The guy said, "Why?" Burton said, "Mort is rare. He's not burdened like the rest of us actors with the words of an author—the words are his own." I would have liked it better if the author hadn't been Shakespeare.

When Newman and I would go to Westport, we would sit around there and he would ask me when I was going to stop chasing rainbows, forget about money, and get down to the real values. And keep drinking. It's compensatory the way some people drink: you're not talking to the same guy by the end of the afternoon. It's kind of like living in America. You're not living in the same country you were born in.

I was back in Hollywood after that. I played a dinner at Romanoff's (Dana Wynter's wedding party, in fact). Jerry Wald was there and he offered me a movie called *In Love and War*, with Jeff Hunter and Robert Wagner, and he asked me to write my own part—which really became a curse in the years to come. And I did. The line I wrote for the picture that broke everybody up at the time was where I picked up a field telephone in Guadalcanal and said, "Good morning, World War II." Groucho Marx even said it was his line. Actually it was out of the folklore of the Aleutian Islands, where I spent several years in the Air Force.

Jerry Wald liked me, and when he produced the Academy Award show in 1960 he made me one of the emcees, along with Bob Hope, Laurence Olivier, Jerry Lewis, and Tony Randall. We all wore tails at the Pantage's Theatre, but the only ones who owned tails were Clark Gable and David Niven. Everybody else had to rent a tuxedo at Dedrick's on Melrose, which is where high school kids go for the prom. I went down there with Bill Holden and John Wayne. Wayne kept taking out a bottle of Jack Daniel's. He turned to me at one point and said, "Why don't you have a drink." And I said, "I can't. I have mononucleosis." So he said to me, "Well, you're OK except for one thing—you don't drink enough."

Then we went to do the show. Hope told the audience, "Later on you'll see Mort Sahl, the favorite comedian of nuclear physicists everywhere." Dean Martin and Sophia Loren introduced me as a comedian who was breaking in his evening clothes as well as his new material. And then I came on and talked about a New York actor who comes to Hollywood and stays at the Chateau Marmont Hotel and never goes out. He says to the manager of the hotel, "I'd like to go out, but if people could go out on the street and see you, they wouldn't pay to see you in the theater." Later, he goes to the Hughes Market across the street, which is open twenty-four hours, and buys some Woolite to rinse his socks in the sink with and a Coke and some instant coffee and Pream. And the clerk says, "Wouldn't you like to take a six-pack?" And the actor says, "Well, I'd like to, but I might be going back to New York." And the routine ended up with General MacArthur walking on the water to reach Corregidor.

The next day Hedda Hopper said in her syndicated column that I was un-American. And she kept that up. She even printed that she had gone to Tom Moore, the head of ABC, the man I worked for, and demanded that he fire me. She admitted that. Which isn't the worst. The worst is that no one was offended.

Gene Norman used to come into the Crescendo about ten or eleven o'clock every night, after I was on and had done the first show. Hanging around me, by osmosis he decided he wanted to go around with actresses. I introduced him to Jean Seberg. Seberg had just broken up with Paul Desmond and they had been through a great situation. He met her when she was seventeen. One time they were out on June 6 and Desmond said, "God, it's the anniversary of D-day." And she said, "Is that the day they bombed Pearl Harbor?" And he said, "No, that's the day they invaded France." And she said, "Well, I never was very good in history." And he realized that he was not very good at child molesting. Anyway, I would come in and say, "How did your date go, Gene?" and he'd say, "Well, I like this girl, but I think she lacks specific gravity." That's what I like about intellectuals: they can always find a way out, but they can never find a way in. "Intellectual" is used facetiously by me and used in error by everyone else. An intellectual is J. Robert Oppenheimer, a Renaissance man. An original thinker. Not a C student who manipulates words.

Intellectualism covers a lot of crimes. The women who wouldn't deliever anything in the feminine sense would make you believe it was because they were intellectuals. It's like when you don't love a girl and never show her any affection because of the strain of the office. It's for people who aren't alive, but then, being alive all the time

73

isn't a hell of a lot like what it appears to be. And all the ex-communist writers who walk around Hollywood with the gray hair and handlebar mustaches tell you they have just been to a sensitivity group. What is a man sixty years old doing up there? Well, he's doing that instead of doing what he should be doing, which is writing a screenplay that expresses his rage about Vietnam. They pretend they're waiting for the moment.

That's why I like Bob Hope. He believes in something and isn't waiting to see which way the wind blows and then get on board. That's the difference between Bob Hope and Jack Webb. Bob Hope created the form and Jack Webb tries to milk it. The road company of a conservative. I don't need the road company, I got tickets to the original.

One time I was going through Texas on a college-tour circuit and Steve McQueen said to stop in to see him and Peckinpah. They were shooting *The Getaway*. And I got to San Marcos, Texas. Jim Garner had also stopped in to see Steve, and they had just done a car stunt in the picture for laughs. He was talking about losing his television series. They were standing in a field in the middle of Texas. McQueen said, "Failure's good. It develops a man's mettle. You show me a man who hasn't failed in some way, and I'll show you a guy who isn't strong. Look at me, I made a movie called *Le Mans* and it only made $15 million." And he said, "Everybody's fallen on his ass and has risen to be a better man." McQueen looked around the field for an example. I was standing there. He said, "Look at Mort."

I love the way they always find me to be the average man. I'm the worst example of anything you want to cite. I'm the exception to every rule. And I'm here for more than to prove it. The disturbing aspect of life to me has always been that everything I prize is intangible. That choice of optimism instead of moral ambiguity defines my journey, which otherwise would be free fall. I've been kept alive for years by the umbilical cord of Frank Capra's movies. My eyes get moist when I watch *Mr. Smith Goes to Washington,* and I realize what they've done to this country since then. Oh, I mean it's vivid to me, but that's totally dependent on my senses. Not the senses that a doctor chronicles, but the private senses which when cultivated give the individual a choice. And there's a war on your senses at all times. The war of desensitization. Art has been desensitized as well as the news. There are movies that show love, which is the only help. The violence and negation in modern films has been misinterpreted as self-indulgence on the part of the artist. They are in fact an index of the audience's dormant or latent mood. Some movies made today could have won at the film festival in Berlin in 1933.

I went to the kids when no one went. I did the first college concert in the United States in 1953 with Dave Brubeck. There is no humorist working who goes to colleges except me. I've often gone cross-country both ways in one day. For a while it was the only audience available to me, and I thought it was important to tell young people that everyone twice their age is not corrupt. I did that. Alone. And, as I'll explain later, I did it for a time with a broken back, in a full brace, from my crotch to my throat. I accused the CIA of murder, but I was driving down the lonely roads to the airports for Flagstaff, Arizona, and Manchester, New Hampshire. I write to you as a man whose conscience is totally out of control.

There was me on the campuses, and there was Gloria Steinem. In 1958, as an employee of *Help* magazine, she came to Los Angeles. And she wiggled around, and I asked her out, and we dated for some time in Los Angeles and New York, but I found something missing. I couldn't get it turned on; but in those days, I was almost enough for both of us. You know the American male—goes off at eight looking for love and by eleven or twelve he becomes discouraged and settles for sensuality. Later on I saw Gloria write for *Harper's Bazaar* "How to Get an Even Tan." She calls herself a writer. I don't know how that would compare with *Principia Mathematica*. I saw her use Mike Nichols. Women using men as stepping stones—all the things she condemns.

And Gloria became a professional liberal. That's easy for a Jewish girl from Cleveland whose father was a junk dealer and who went to Smith College. In fact, if you have that catalogue from Smith handy, I'll wait while you look up the requirements.

When I was in New York I was with Herb Gardner, who was a friend of Herb Sargent and Marlo Thomas, and they really embraced me. Eventually the subject of Gloria came up. What do you think of Gloria? And I said, "You better keep your opinion of Gloria and not solicit mine, because it may erode our relationship." No, they've gotta know. So I told 'em. And Marlo said, "We're doing important work. Gloria had me go to Doubleday today and get a children's book out. You know, the one that says, 'Bob is a pilot and Jane is a stewardess.' This is chauvinistic and it must be removed from the shelves." Herb said, comparing me to Gloria, "You're worse than she is." I said, "How?" And he said, "Because you won't give a person amnesty. She made a mistake, and now it's over." And I said, "Yeah, it's like those fellas who used to work for the Mafia but don't anymore." I believe in redemption.

Actors know about spontaneous feelings. When they have to improvise, the guys slap girls and the girls cry. And I knew all about acting classes. At one time Newman said I had to study because he had studied at the Actors Studio, and Joanne had studied with Sandy Meisner at the Neighborhood Playhouse. So Meisner came to Hollywood and set up a class at Twentieth Century Fox. Joanne enrolled in the class. That was reverse snobbery. You get a million and a half dollars per picture, but you go to class and you return to New York and you do plays—in dirty theaters if possible. So she asked me to be her partner in class.

We enrolled in Meisner's class. It was really something. The first thing you had to do was wind watches or open doors. It's called an exercise with inanimate objects. And I worked with a lot of inanimate objects, but space does not permit my listing all those actors. Meisner threw me out of the class. He said, "You've already developed your character." It's the same as Gregory Peck playing himself or Audrey Hepburn playing herself. He said he didn't want to tamper with it because it's been successful on the stage. He said he could teach me not to verbalize as much, but he didn't want to alter it. He also threw Dennis Hopper out of the class once, because of a scene centered on a plane leaving an island with only ten seats, for which twenty passengers are competing. How do you, improvising, convince them that you have to get on? So, Dennis went over and pounded on the door and said, "I've gotta get on. I've gotta get on." And they asked why and he said, "Because I'm the pilot." He was thrown out for being facetious.

Cloris Leachman told me once that she was in the Actors Studio in New York and a guy was doing a sensory exercise of peeling a banana. And he was so intense that she literally could smell the banana. She thought it was a fantastic experience until she turned around and saw the guy behind her eating a banana, watching the same scene.

Cloris Leachman was married to George Englund. Englund came on the set when she and I made a television pilot together because he thought that someone was running away with his wife. The irony was that I became fast friends with him. Englund used to travel with a dictionary at his elbow. He liked nothing better than to meet actors and use words that they didn't understand, which isn't really an Olympic competition against actors. The last time I saw him he'd become a stockbroker. And I said something about Nixon during the Watergate period. We were at a party surrounded by stockbrokers. He said, "Don't say that." During the Kennedy years, he came to know Shriver. And he kept saying to me, "Your era is coming." He was like a lot of people in Hollywood—didn't want to get too close for fear of getting burned, but they didn't want to count me out because I just might win.

I saw Stevenson again in Chicago and we had a reception at Bill Blair's apartment and Adlai said to me, "I've been talking to Kennedy and I think he has merit. The Old Man is going to make a big push, although," he said, "if this young man emerges, it'll be the winds of fate." I said, "You know, either that, or the Old Man sitting at the back of the auditorium with a bellows." Well, he ignored that and he said to me, "Well, at least Jack and Bobby are in this century. The Kennedy girls are like Irishwomen out of the 1800's."

I was working the Chez Paree, and Stevenson came in one night with the editor of the London *Economist,* Barbara Ward (Lady Jackson), and we were talking about socialism. She was telling me that Americans don't understand that when England nationalized the coal mines, they had no choice: it was economic survival. Americans always act like people had opted for slavery. She started talking about Castro, and Sargent Shriver and his wife, Eunice Kennedy, were at the table. He was then running the Chicago School Board. Eunice said, "You know, I think we should bomb the hell out of Castro," etc. Barbara Ward called her a fascist and Eunice said, "That's right." Later, Eunice Shriver was saying things to me in Chicago like "You must come to the White House." And I said, "Why, is Adlai going to stop there soon?" And she'd say, "I mean, when my brother is President of the United States."

And of course I was getting the stereo version, because the other speaker, on the West Coast, was Pat Lawford. I was still going out with Phyllis, and we were going to dinner at Lawford's house at the beach, and I'd been making a joke about Jack: If he doesn't get nominated, he can go back to Harvard and write a term paper called "What I Did on My Summer Vacation." Pat said, "I don't think that's funny." Pat would also say things like "My brother is the most important thing in my life," which wouldn't matter if she hadn't had four children and a husband. Lawford would go up to the movies at Sinatra's house, and at five o'clock in the morning when Pat would say she wanted to go home, he would tell her to take the other car and go home, because he was going to stay until Frank dismissed the audience.

In New York I was working at Basin Street, and Milt Ebbins and I were sitting in the Essex House one day and Joe Cates came to see him. He had just done a television special with me for Pontiac on NBC and he had done *The $64,000 Question*. Ebbins claimed he told Cates he could be a help if there were any legal questions about *The $64,000 Question*. There were people identified in the hall who Ebbins assured me were from Frank Hogan's D.A. Office for the purpose of taping the conversation. All this fascinated Ebbins; it was extracurricular power play. He wasn't too interested in show business. I helped to provide a steady income so he could pursue his avocation.

The next thing I knew I got a telephone call. Ebbins

said, "It's important." I took the receiver. "This is Ambassador Joseph Kennedy. I understand that you're preeminent in the field of political humor. I want you to write some things for Johnny." I said, "Well, I'll be happy to, but understand I don't endorse candidates." "I'm not interested in who you endorse; I want you to do this." I said, "Fine," and I started writing the material, and I gave it to whoever came for it. I gave it to Pat Lawford, who was a courier on the West Coast. Kennedy's private plane, the *Caroline*, stopped a couple of times in New York and Ted Sorensen or Pierre Salinger arrived to pick up the material. Even when I was on location in Montana making *All the Young Men*, I borrowed the sheriff's Jeep and drove from Hungry Horse to Helena, to Western Union, to send a wire to Senator John Kennedy at the Senate Office Building containing material, a lot of which was on Eisenhower (which he never used, I might add).

I suggested he say that if the Pope called him John, he should call the Pope Jack. Or, he tell the Baptist convention in Houston, "It's not the hereafter that bothers me, but the November election is driving me out of my head." And when I left to go to Russia (this was a trip about which Adlai Stevenson said, after giving me a letter to Khrushchev, "This man has just returned from the Soviet Union while Premier Khrushchev was in New York. I don't know who won more points, but I know who won more hearts.") I stopped in the departure lounge at Idlewild to wire more material to Kennedy. I did all this on the fly, at odd hours.

Kennedy came to Los Angeles to ask for the California delegation votes. I was shooting the interiors for the movie at Columbia. The night before, I had been at La Scala with Dyan Cannon, eating dinner. A car drove up, a black

Ghia (Sinatra bought it with the proviso that the dealer would not sell another black one in the continental United States). Sinatra, who had vowed he'd never come into La Scala (one of his many life decisions), came inside with Dean Martin, drew up a table. "Mort, I need your help. I want you to write some material for me. I'm going to be working with Jack Kennedy and I'd really appreciate it." And I took it on with all the enthusiasm of Conrak teaching a class of illiterates. So I started writing his material along with Jack's.

At the banquet at the Beverly Hilton with Governor Brown and Senator Kennedy, where I was the emcee, I had to make sure I didn't duplicate the same jokes I had given Kennedy and Sinatra. The banquet was at 8:30, and James Darren and I were shooting a scene from the movie in which we're in a machine-gun nest in Korea and he's got a trained frog and he wants it to jump and it won't jump. We shot the scene *thirty-six* times. And it's getting to be 9:15. And I said, "I've got to go." And the director, Hal Bartlett, said, "It isn't right, it isn't right." And finally he said to me, "Whether the scene is right is kind of immaterial, as I happen to be on the other side; I'm a Republican."

So then I went to the dinner. It was the first time I met Kennedy, standing there with those laser-beam blue eyes, looking very quizzical. He was curious about me, my age, my political posture. Shook hands, told me he appreciated what I was doing, and asked, "Have you got any more one-liners? This looks like a rough crowd." Bobby just sat on the sidelines and waited. I suppose that even though he was emotionally as loyal as he was to his brother, he was waiting his turn. In the crevices of his mind he was a lot like Hamlet. He must have wondered why it was his lot in life to break the doors down for this guy and to cut all the corners and be an outlaw of sorts and then be re-

81

warded by people saying, "Jack, you're great, but I can't stand that rat who works for you." There had to be a jealousy—which I thought he contained admirably.

Afterward, we went to Kennedy's plane, parked at L.A. International Airport. He was on his way to Palm Springs with Sinatra and he called me to join him on the plane. When I got aboard he asked me to sit up front. The Senator said, "Where was Paul Ziffren four years ago?" I said, "I guess with Stevenson." He said, "Of course, a logical position," and I said, "How do you arrive at a logical position?" and he said, "You just think in terms of survival." Everybody was drinking Bloody Marys. Then Kennedy put his finger to his forehead, pensively, and he said, "Tell me, why do you like Castro?" He never let his ego stand in the way of his curiosity. I told him of my admiration for Castro and that a revolutionary, I thought, appealed to all Americans—well, not quite all, for Americans view South American revolutionaries as a joke, the Russian revolutionaries as a horror, and the American revolutionaries as heroes.

Kennedy asked me about a joke I told on television about him. He was grilling me, knowing the answers, but insisting on my telling them to him literally. I had said on TV that his father had said, "I'm putting you on an allowance. You're not allowed one more cent than you need to buy a landslide." "What does that mean?" Kennedy asked, relentlessly. I told him it meant his father was rich, for one thing. "How much do you think he has?" he asked. So I made a snap decision and said, "Four hundred million." He looked at me as if I were retarded and asked if I knew how much the Rockefeller brothers were worth. "Liquid," he said, "about ten billion." Then he looked at me and said, "Now, that's money!"

My first convention had been the 1958 Republican convention in San Francisco. I had appeared there on CBS's

Morning Show, which was the Will Rogers show out of the Mark Hopkins, across the street from the *Today* show with Dave Garroway, which was coming out of the Fairmont. We opened the show live for New York, which meant 4:00—with the time differential, 4:00 in the morning. It was pitch black in San Francisco. I rode in on a fire truck. It was the producer's idea. We were trying to act festive and happy. Television is never more false than when it's openly sincere.

In 1960, I was on Channel 9 in Los Angeles. I essentially did the program myself. It was sponsored by Bart Lytton, who had opened Lytton Savings & Loan on the site of the former Garden of Allah Hotel and was self-described as perpetual sponsor of the Democratic Party. He was a sort of Madman Muntz of finance who had been chartered in Nevada, and that will give you an idea of his stability and fiduciary integrity. Whenever there was a Democratic dinner in Los Angeles, he was on a dais next to people like Mrs. Roosevelt. In fact, I eventually saw Kennedy taking Lytton's calls instead of talking to those who had prior call on his time, the leaders of the emerging African nations. So the guy swung with some financial weight. What other kind is there in politics? He himself had half a delegate vote as a Chester Bowles delegate to the Democratic Convention.

I went on the air, and everybody who was at the convention would drop in. I had on Ted Kennedy, who was a twenty-nine-year-old courier for his brother, and Governor LeRoy Collins of Florida, and Larry O'Brien and Drew Pearson and Jack Anderson. We broke a lot of ground on the show because anything went. One night Irv Kupcinet from Chicago was on with Bill Dana and anybody else who happened to drop in. And I had just come back from the convention, and Eugene McCarthy had said to the convention, "Do not turn your back on Adlai Stevenson."

Mrs. Roosevelt was there to back him up. It was a ground swell. Bobby was really worried that he couldn't hold his thumb in the dike for Jack's candidacy. And, of course, the convention was reasonably rigged. I mean, rigged not to accept a ground swell for Stevenson. Because, you know, Bobby had twenty-three telephones and air-conditioned headquarters, while Stevenson was trying to negotiate a GI loan to get a garage in back of the Sports Arena. And Stevenson wasn't actively pushing his candidacy. But McCarthy was. He thought it was the party's last chance. And the Kennedy candidacy almost fell through that night. I mean, people just wouldn't keep quiet.

While I was broadcasting, Bart Lytton, in his white dinner jacket, with a carnation in his lapel and a white Cadillac with gold wheels and Maserati air horns on the fender, drove up to the bank, past the security guard and the electric fence, and drove through the wooden fence with the horns blaring, ran upstairs while I was on the air on the second floor of the bank, in front of the camera, and said, "I'm not running a Stevenson rally."

Well, that night I was watching NBC News and Chet Huntley said, "While Fidel Castro was castigating Franco's Spain, he was interrupted on the air in the studio by the presence on camera of the Spanish ambassador, who protested his remarks, and Castro banished him from the country, revoking his credentials." He continued, "Nothing like that has happened in modern history," And David Brinkley said, "I beg to differ, Chet. Bart Lytton walked in on Mort Sahl tonight, at least as portentous an event." All this later made *Time* magazine. So Lytton called me up and said, "People are withdrawing money from the bank. You should see the letters." One of them was from Steve Allen; he was withdrawing $10,000, citing that he felt Lytton was not stable enough to be the custodian of his funds. And he said to me, "This thing is hurting now but will be good publicity in the long run." There is no heroism in American commerce. When you try to put a premium on self-respect, they want to pay the premium.

When people reject you, often you have made that your own choice. When the door is closed, you have bolted it from the other side. I can take this all the way to the level of the President of the United States. I served notice on Kennedy that I was going to attack him, and *he* didn't reject me. The core of neurosis is to think people ostracize you after you've submitted your resignation. Talking to Kennedy after he was elected and telling him you're not coming to dinner and you're going to go your own way is Marlon Brando's confrontation with Karl Malden in *One-Eyed Jacks*. They had been bank robbers together, but now Malden is the sheriff. The bank robber looks at the sheriff and says, "I'm still in business."

At the second convention, 1960, Kennedy was nominated and now it fell to the convention to choose a Vice President. I was at the Biltmore Hotel, where Sam Rayburn told Johnson, "You're no son of mine if you accept second place. You have to go all the way." Johnson was visited by H. L. Hunt, which has since been documented but certainly wasn't underlined by them at the time. Bobby went downstairs reluctantly, on the orders of his father and Jack, to offer the job to Johnson. And Johnson accepted. And Rayburn walked in and said, "You're not even a man." And Johnson threw himself across the bed and was racked by sobs. Bobby kept saying to Jack, "Take Johnson: you will only lose every labor vote, every Northern city vote, every Jew and Negro in every metropolitan city." Bobby had promised the Vice Presidency to nine people that I knew of.

Bobby was uncomfortable in the whole Hollywood milieu. Jack was always curious about people in the arts and would have been a movie producer had he lived to enjoy his retirement.

After I made the *Time* cover, I built up a liaison with Henry Luce and he took me a lot of places—for instance, seminars. He came to Los Angeles once, and he was transferring the head of the Detroit bureau to replace the head of the Los Angeles bureau, who was becoming an editor of the L.A. *Times*. So he took the occasion to have one of his all-male dinners at Perino's. All the dinosaurs were there, the Regents of USC, Art Linkletter, George Stevens, and some bosses from Occidental Oil. Luce got up and he said, "The first thing I want tonight is a little brainstorming," he said. Stimulus. "I want to state that we can't afford a mistake in America. So if this young Kennedy makes a mistake, he's got to be impeached immediately. We can't wait for a second. It's too crucial." And nobody differed with him. Then he said, "I wanna welcome our new editor of the L.A. bureau, Frank McCulloch, who has been transferred here from Detroit." The news that week was that a Chrysler executive had been accused of taking kickbacks. So Luce said, "He did a thorough job in Detroit, everyone will agree, even our resident iconoclast, Mr. Sahl." So I said, "How thoroughly did he cover Chrysler while he was there?" And Luce said to the audience, "No major publication in America exists without automobile advertising. Integrity is a word I left at Yale."

Much later, there was a fortieth anniversary party for *Time* cover subects. Luce was getting on in years and he said he might not see the fiftieth year. So he decided to fly everybody to the Waldorf for a command performance dinner. And everybody was there who'd been on the cover, you know, with the exception of Calvin Coolidge and Woodrow Wilson and Warren G. Harding. I was sitting at a table with the likes of Dave Brubeck, Jack Paar, Bette Davis, General Curtis LeMay, Barry Goldwater,

Jacob Javits, and Lillian Hellman. Luce said, "How do you like the party?" I said, "You know, if a bomb fell on this building, our society could get off to a fresh start." Luce went down to make the opening remarks and he introduced the noted theologian Paul Tillich, and Tillich went to the blackboard and wrote, "Man equals God." And as an old math major from Berkeley, I can tell you that that equation is not in balance, especially if you transpose it.

I don't believe that anyone is above humor. I think you can talk about the Chief Justice and I think you can talk about the President. I once had dinner with Nixon, and he encouraged me to do it as a matter of fact. Nixon was once quoted in *Time* as saying that I'm the Will Rogers of our time. There's quite a bit of difference between Rogers and me. Rogers came on the stage and impersonated a yokel who was critical of the federal government. And when I come on the stage, I impersonate an intellectual who is critical of yokels who are running the federal government. Other than that, we're similar in every respect.

I'll tell you about the time I met Nixon. I had gone into La Scala with Paul Newman. Nixon had just failed in his bid for the governorship of California and was sitting there with his wife and a contractor. The guy had built a stadium some miles away, which was, at the time, I think, collapsing because the concrete was diluted. So Newman said to me, "Why don't you buy him a drink? You've mocked him so much, why don't you meet him?" So I sent Nixon a note and I said I'd like to buy him a drink. He sent me back a note saying, "I'll have wine with you, if you'll join us." That's how I verified that it was really Nixon, it wasn't astigmatism. Because he couldn't just have a drink; he had to make a deal.

I went over to the table and I introduced myself and

sat down. The wine steward came over and asked what Nixon had ordered to eat. Nixon said cottage cheese and meat loaf. The wine steward asked what wine he would like to go with that. Nixon said, "What would you recommend?" I thought it was a toss-up between Ripple and Thunderbird, but the guy said, "Well, Mr. Nixon, how about the Rothschild?" Nixon said, "No, we're going to have an American wine." He was very adamant.

The wine steward blanched because he saw his money going out the window. He said, "What year?" Nixon said, "This year." So the guy was really dying now. And Nixon said to him, "Why don't you bring it right up with dinner?" So, we had the wine, and when the dinner was over, he said, "Don't forget to keep a candle under my ass, and under Kennedy's too. It's good for America. You're the Will Rogers of our time." So I said, "How do I know you haven't said that to Bob Hope?" And then the check came, and I grabbed it. Women don't know about that. That's the last test of virility left. Because the frontiers are gone. Alaska's gone, and you can't outdraw people in frontier towns. That's all there is left.

I reached for the check, and Nixon reached for it too. It was a battle of wits. I finally got it. I paid with Diners Club. The captain stamped the card, and, you know, it has on it the tab, and gratuities, and tax, and FICA, and W-S, and withholding, and United Nations payments, and deficits, and devaluation of the dollar, and on the back you have to write down whether it is a deductible dinner. So, as a test of the law, I wrote that it was a business dinner and my guests were Mr. and Mrs. Richard M. Nixon. It asked, "Did you discuss specific business?" And I said, "Yes, we discussed excessive taxation and the possible overthrow of the United States Government." I later mailed that receipt in with my copy of my IRS return and wondered whether the computers would jam up at the audit center for the Internal Revenue Service in Westport, Connecticut.

Kennedy was elected by one-tenth of 1 percent of the vote, counting Texas and Cook County. And then the rewards began to be handed out. Adlai Stevenson left his law firm to become ambassador to the United Nations. William McCormick Blair left Stevenson's law firm to become ambassador to Denmark. Bill Rivkin became ambassador to Luxembourg. Willard Wirtz, same law office, became Secretary of Labor, Under-Secretary first. Newton Minow became head of the FCC. So you see, virtue is not its own reward. Everybody had to get something, although they said they were all doing it altruistically. Sinatra got to plan the Gala. They had a big dinner and show in the Armory in Washington to celebrate the victory, which I was not invited to. My manager, Milt Ebbins, was on his way to Washington with Lawford for the Gala, Ebbins carrying Frank Sinatra's golf clubs. They all went to Washington. Nobody ever said thank you to me. Before Jack became President, we were having our picture taken together, which he was going to autograph, and the photographer asked me to wave my finger in what he said was a typical Mort Sahl gesture, you know. Right, and the President refused to sign the picture. He said, "See anything wrong with this picture?" And I said, "No, what?" And he said, "Shouldn't you be listening to me?"

So the Kennedys started ruling and I started attacking them. It was reported to me by Ebbins that my detrimental humor had gotten back to the President, and his intimates had referred to me as "that bastard," and the President agreed but said, "He's a smart bastard." He always wanted to know what the enemy was thinking.

America had a new optimism. People today say it was a little more than optimism, and that we don't know how the President would have worked out—he didn't live long enough. Nowadays we find that optimism is extremely tangible, now that we know what it's like to live without any.

One night he came into the Crescendo and I had just had dinner with Marilyn Monroe. She was at odds with herself and didn't know what to do. So I said, "Well, listen, you were married to Joe DiMaggio and Arthur Miller. I think the only thing left now is to marry Adlai Stevenson." And she laughed. I came down to the club that night. Kennedy was in the audience in the back booth. And I said, "I have a bulletin. Marilyn Monroe is going to marry Adlai Stevenson. Now, Kennedy can be jealous of him twice." And I heard a fist come down on the table and a voice in New England dialect saying, "God damn it." Even though I knew Marilyn for a long time, she forgot.

It was John Huston's birthday when they were filming *The Misfits* with Clark Gable and Marilyn Monroe in Reno, and they asked me to come up and entertain at a birthday party for Huston. And I flew up there and Huston was drunk, and he introduced me to Marilyn, whom I'd known for years. And she was drunk, and she took my hand and put it right on her breast and she said, "Don't be afraid, Mr. Sahl." And I said, "I'm not afraid." And she said, "How wrong you are. We're all afraid."

Bill Blair was invited down to Lawford's house that week when Stevenson had refused to endorse any candidate. (He thought it was an open convention, of course.) As Blair walked into Lawford's house, Old Man Kennedy ran his cane across his chest and he said, "What's the matter with your man [Stevenson], is he crazy?" Both Bobby and the Old Man were very busy getting into office so they could get even. And Pat Lawford had the same nature. Jack had not. Jack was the man who said, "Life is not fair." He said it often, and always wistfully, recognizing that America was full of people who weren't forty-two and President. I know that life's not fair, but I never asked it to be. A man isn't entitled to anything except something to believe in.

Ebbins and Lawford began to commute now to Washington, and Lawford's living was a mystery to me. Ebbins told everyone that United Artists, at the request of Joseph Kennedy, established ChrisLaw Productions and gave Lawford *The Patty Duke Show* to produce, although the show was done in New York and Lawford was in California. And he suddenly had an office; he took Sinatra's old office on the top of the William Morris Agency and sat up there. Joseph Kennedy was often on the phone to Peter. I'd hear the Old Man on the phone saying, "Peter, did you get the part you wanted? No? Well, I told you never to do business with Jews," or "Dissolve your restaurant partnership with Sinatra." Or I'd walk in and hear arrangements being made for the President's entertainment. I heard a lot of girls named. They were fond of saying: "Number One is coming to town." Sometimes it was so indiscreet it was done out loud. I never objected to the President's private life; his public acts are open to scrutiny of course. There's a difference. The recruitment of Marilyn Monroe for Kennedy's birthday party was done by Ebbins and Lawford. She was making a picture at Fox called *Something's Gotta Give*. They had a helicopter waiting on the lot which took her to the airport for the flight to New York. Her absence resulted in her suspension from her last movie. When the President was in Palm Springs, Milt Ebbins was carrying the fettucini from La Scala's to a chartered plane at Clover Field in Santa Monica. Dignity, all the way.

91

Ebbins used to return from Washington or Palm Springs or visit Lawford's home in Malibu and he'd say to me, "They squeezed me at dinner: the Old Man said, 'Doesn't Sahl know the meaning of the word loyalty?'" He would tell them he could get me to stop doing it. And every time he brought that up, I would react by doing three times as much material. And he'd come back and he'd tell me all the time, "They said you're not loyal, the Old Man said you're not loyal," and I said, "You're trying to tell me that the man who faced the Cuban missile crisis and the problems of the Berlin Wall is worried about a nightclub comedian. I find that hard to accept, even with my ego." And Ebbins would say, "Well, I would sure like to get you together with Jack. I think if you'd come out to the plane one time . . . I'll arrange it, because I think you could talk your problems out." We had now established that we had problems. He acted like it was the Moscow summit. And Lawford would say to me, "If you could only be reasonable, you could be a king." Be a king like Lawford, about whom the President objected because Lawford asked the Secret Service men to carry his bags, and who was banished by the President once because he played golf on the White House lawn in bare feet.

For some reason Ebbins stayed very close to Lawford. He never had any money. I advanced Ebbins the money. I gave him a car on his birthday, and I advanced him the money to buy his house. My business manager took a note on it, but I never intended to collect it. And Ebbins was never present at a single engagement I had on the road. Ebbins just kept pounding away saying, "People don't want to hear that about the President. You know Jack thought you were for him; he's really hurt." And so one day when I walked across to Hamburger Hamlet on Beverly Drive from the Morris office, I found Lawford and Ebbins on the sidewalk, yelling at me, "The ambassador says if you don't cooperate, you'll never work again in the United States."

Then the work began to dry up. I'd gone down to the office every day. No work. That's kind of funny. In time I heard that Lou Morheim wanted me for a film based on his novel but the Morris office wouldn't give him a meeting. Paramount Pictures was told that I wasn't available because I was seeing a psychiatrist seven days a week. Other people were told I was physically ill and that's why I had removed myself. I was losing my access.

The Crescendo was sold by Gene Norman to Shelley Davis, a press agent. Davis was man enough to tell me what was happening. He said, "I've been told that the White House would be offended if I hired you and I'd be audited on my income tax. I heard that you offended the President." He didn't want to know how or when. He just knew it.

I tried to retrace my steps. I went back to every club where I used to work but nothing was available at any price. It didn't make sense. I was at a point where I was offering third-grade nightclub operators the chance to make money. I was indemnifying them by working for practically nothing. And they were not interested. The Morris office wasn't interested in booking me and eventually wasn't interested in representing me. Sam Weisbord said to me, "You've built up too much animus and you've destroyed our office." Well, you know, that's like Hitler saying, "The last American tourist destroyed Berlin."

Sinatra said to me, "I'm forever in your debt for what you did writing the material for the campaign." He used to call me when I was on the road. When he wanted to talk I'd be at some place like the University of Minnesota, or the University of Wisconsin, and he'd call me for help from the Sands in Vegas. He once called and said he needed me to open at the Fontainebleau because the show was in trouble. When he wanted some lines between songs for the stage, he'd ask me to write the material. Once, he put his arm around me and said, "You're a rebel; I'm a rebel. I'm really your brother. There are no other rebels." And he said, "If you ever have a problem and you don't come to me first, I'll break both your arms." When he started the record company, he said, "I want you on the label." The first album was "The New Frontier," the first album to satirize the Kennedy administration.

What was my role at this time? In America there was optimism—we owe that to Kennedy—and there were a lot of bright people ready to work in government. But Kennedy needed, the country needed, a defined political opposition that was at least as sophisticated as the New Frontiersmen. It needed this because Kennedy's election was an opportunity, not an accomplishment, as Schlesinger and Sorensen later came to describe it. I believed America's promise is a chance.

A lot of what I heard from politicians has nothing to do with what people think are political issues. Take my theory about the social democrats. Red, yellow, and black. Black for fascism, of course. Red for communism. That only leaves yellow for social democrats—gosh, I always though it was a choice. It became evident to me along the way that the sellout was that of the social democrats. And, of course, I use the term as it is used in Germany or the Scandinavian countries.

Social democrats are everywhere, and they can destroy the country. A social democratic President would have to bomb China to prove he's not a communist.

The impact that George Wallace had was because of

his conviction. The liberal candidates have no conviction. If you've got John Wayne's handshake on something, you can put it in the bank. Don't give me Pierre Salinger.

There are the people who throw their hands up and say to you, "Well, I hope you understand, Mort, why I'm turning you in." The value of a conservative—not a fascist—is that if you illuminate him with new information, he may move to a new position as a result of that illumination. Not so with the liberals who are social democrats but not radicals. Any man with passion, with a heart, is a left-wing social democrat. A good indication of the condition of this country is that there's nothing on the horizon left of right-wing social democrats.

There are three categories of social democrats: the left wing, the right wing, and the middle. Now, the people who come out of college are usually leftists, but they're afraid to lose their jobs. They don't want to become rightists because they're not dedicated enough to get a uniform and attend meetings regularly. So, what they do is become social democrats and talk to their black maid while she's sweeping: "Dolores, how's your son doing at community college running the drill press?"

Now for a finer gradation. Among the left-wingers there are right-wing left-wingers. The left wing of the left wing said about Vietnam, "The Americans have got to get out before there are any talks." The middle-of-the-road left wing said, "I wish I had said that." And the right wing of left wing, which was the Russian position, said, "There should be talks, but they can't be between the North and South; they're too close to the problem. It's got to be between the major powers." The left-wing social democrat said, "Well, I don't like it any better than you do, but there are eight hundred million of 'em, Ted. Let's get another drink. . . ."

Enver Hoxha, the premier of Albania, is a left-wing

95

left-winger, a soul-searching man. Castro is the middle-of-the-road of the left. Brezhnev is in the right wing of the left wing. William O. Douglas is a left-wing social democrat.

Right-wing social democrats are really overstaffed. Proxmire, Javits, Lindsay, Humphrey, Paul Newman, Marlon Brando, Charlton Heston, Steve Allen, Kim Novak. Anyone who manipulates the hearts and minds of millions.

A middle-of-the-road fascist is usually anybody who's wait-listed to be a right-wing fascist. That would be J. Edgar Hoover, when he was with us. By the way, where is Ted Kennedy? He's above the whole chart. He's circling, waiting to be cleared for a landing.

Basically, in other words, the left is made up of the SDS. And the right is made up of the Board of GM, the CIA, and the AMA.

Social democrats also write television shows. Almost to the exclusion of everyone else. You know the kind of shows. Our daughter is fifteen and she's pregnant. She *failed* us. And the hero's a social democrat. He says, "Mr. Simpson, *she* failed?" That's social democracy. The science-fiction picture: if a monster chews up the city and we think it's our fault for driving him to it, that's social democracy. They have no one else to punish. Victims are always in short supply. Even though there are many volunteers.

I finally got my visit to the White House. One day I took my dad there. The last time he'd been in Washington was thirty years before, as a clerk at the VA. He'd never been on a jet. So we took off on United, we saw the movie. I got him a panatela; he had the steak. We landed in Washington, and the next day I called the White House and Jack Valenti answered. He asked my dad and me to come over to have lunch with him.

The Secret Service let us into the White House. Took

our coats. We ate downstairs in the Navy mess Johnson had put in. Remember, you couldn't go out for lunch, because you'd waste man-hours. The same man who turned out light bulbs, which are a symbol in all comic strips of creative thought. After lunch, Valenti, in his office, unlocked some Cuban cigars and gave my dad one.

Dick Goodwin, who had written speeches for both Kennedy and Johnson, came in and said, "Come on down and visit." So we went to Goodwin's office, and he had a picture of Kennedy up there with "The New Frontier" phrase written in longhand—it had been coined in the Alaskan campaign swing. He had a picture of Mike Nichols and Elizabeth Taylor alongside. Those were Goodwin's priorities. Then we went back into Valenti's office. Goodwin said, "Have you read Mailer's new book? Although," he continued, "I should know better than to ask in the Johnson White House if anybody's read anything."

Then Valenti talked to my dad about Johnson. Told him he was serving even though he'd had two heart attacks. Took my dad and showed him the chair at which he convened his cabinet meetings, the chair that said "Franklin D. Roosevelt" on the back. We walked out of the White House and stood on the sidewalk on Pennsylvania Avenue. Dad said to Valenti, "Please express my respects to President Johnson. The man's given up his health, endangered himself, to serve us." I turned to my dad and said, "Jesus Christ, you're destroying everything I built."

Jack Valenti and I once were on *The Dick Cavett Show* together. I first encountered Cavett, by the way, when he was a junior writer on *The Tonight Show*. Cavett worked in a few nightclubs, and I got him a job on *The Jerry Lewis Show* as a writer. (When he came to California, he was terribly alone. He was married to an actress, which

97

is the same as being alone. The night of a Jerry Lewis premiere show, I was with Yvonne Craig, who later, after I educated her, went to work on *Batman,* which shows that some people are above adult education. She had these long white gloves that went over the elbow, and Cavett was so busy watching the show being screened that while eating Baked Alaska, instead of reaching for his napkin, he took her gloves and wiped his mouth.)

When Jack Valenti and I were on Cavett's show, I spoke about the CIA. During the commercial, Jack leaned over to me and said, "Mort, President Johnson's not responsible. He really doesn't know what those bastards are doing." That was the first admission I had by anyone in the government that they were doing anything. Cavett would say things to me like "I can't bring myself to believe that."

It is a common dilemma. When you're engaged in something that is dramatic and against the common opinion—and even embarrassing to some people—you say, "Well, the times have changed and I've got to take my stand." The funny thing is that other people say, "He's changed. I wonder what happened to him." This difference in view is what took place in 1964, 1965, and 1966 between me and the people who control access to the American audience.

Let's take a step backward. When I introduced political commentary into my humor, making fun of Eisenhower and, later, Stevenson and Kennedy, it was unusual, largely original. I was the first postgraduate humorist, the first witticist comedian. I don't call myself this. The people who came after—Woody Allen, Shelley Berman, Dick Cavett, and the others, in declining order—have at one time or another said that I was the pioneer, the first person to introduce intellectualism into stand-up comic routines, the first American humorist to make iconoclasm capture an audience.

Making fun of the politics of Eisenhower and Stevenson and Kennedy, sharp and incisive though it could be, was still part of the American tradition. Finley Peter Dunne said that Americans build memorial arches to their heroes out of bricks so that they can throw bricks at them after they pass through. I wasn't as bland as Will Rogers or Bob Hope—with them it didn't make any difference whether you say Democrat or Republican; it's the same joke. With me it made a difference whether it was Eisenhower or Stevenson or Kennedy, but even so, I assumed that the targets of my criticism and I could agree on the game itself: we could agree that in the American republic you have choices, and you are allowed to make bad choices without being eternally punished. We could agree that politics was not fatal, however bad it was. So I wasn't Will Rogers, but I wasn't a revolutionary either. I wasn't even Savonarola: I didn't want to punish my fellow Americans.

All that changed dramatically in the mid-'60's. How else can I explain that I spent four years, off and on, working with Jim Garrison on the Kennedy assassination without a cent of salary, with no expense money, all that time being suspected or accused of the most awesome crime of all in the eyes of show business—of not being funny and beloved any longer? My humor didn't stop. It changed. I can still find a lot of examples that are humorous and incisive in politics, especially among the social democrats. But somehow politics isn't as innocent as that now. I found it difficult to write political commentary about Lyndon Johnson and Richard Nixon in the same tone I spoke of Eisenhower, Stevenson, and Kennedy. Bob Hope talked less and less of politics after the mid-'60s. Can you imagine Will Rogers cracking jokes about the Vietnam

War? Can you imagine Will Rogers talking whimsically about the American electorate when neither the President nor the Vice President was elected?

I never complained about what all this cost me. But surely it's not uninteresting to recount that in America a man can go from $600,000 or $1,000,000 a year gross income to $13,000 and still put in more hours on his time-card. It is not paranoia to understand how information and entertainment are dispensed to mass audiences in America. A few scores of people do really decide what goes on networks, what goes over wire services, what appears in news magazines, what appears in mass-market paperback books, what goes on radio. There's nothing wrong with the mechanics. I've never been the simple-minded populist who thinks that all enterprises can be run by everybody. The issue isn't that a few scores of people ultimately control access to the mass audience; that isn't suspect. It's who these people are. Reactionaries in America attack the press because essentially they don't have access to the mass audience. Liberals rarely attack the press in America, because they do have access and they feel virtuous because they once had a flirtation with good intentions.

The question of virtue in the media is a complicated one. Much as I hated Joe McCarthy for what he did, I never felt comfortable that Edward R. Murrow could do a one-hour hatchet job on him with all the liberals cheering. When you asked them, "What if Murrow did that to Stevenson?" the only thing they could say was, "Well, Murrow wouldn't do that."

As a commentator and entertainer who reached millions of people, I have to believe that I earned their attention and kept them interested. I don't think that any twenty thousand people at any one moment are capable of doing that. The real question is, did I at the age of thirty-five suddenly lose my stuff? Did the American public defect en masse?

When did I first begin to recognize my responsibility to America? It is hard to know the exact moment. Maybe it wasn't an event. Maybe it was a moment of realization when a confluence of strange circumstances turned America into a dangerous place. We became dangerous to ourselves. It is the events that showed themselves and the people who did not show themselves. The events appeared. The people disappeared.

What was the confluence of events? The Kennedy assassination. A twenty-six-volume Warren Commission Report that nobody read whole, that contains testimony of only thirty-seven witnesses before the Commission; the work of a Commission that never met as a full body and conducted its hearing generally with only two of the seven members present; that dealt with an autopsy that has never been verified, with a ballistics theory that nobody could confirm and few have since believed.

All this happened when the most obscene event in American history was unfolding—the Vietnam War. It happened when the American electorate was presided over first by a President who succeeded because of an assassination that has never been officially admitted to; then by a President who was removed from office; and then by a President who was not elected and who has just recently been told by his Vice President (who also was not elected)that he does not care to run. (Rockefeller is an ingrate. After all, Ford did appoint him, which is more than Ford can say about Rockefeller.)

How do you characterize this period? If you called it strange, if you called it dangerous, would that make you a bona fide paranoiac?

I have always been sympathetic with hypochondriacs. After all, if you think you're sick, it hurts. I had to live the past ten years with the word "paranoia." But it's a funny thing about people who are discriminated against. Others accuse them of paranoia if the victim happens to notice it. Nobody accused John Henry Faulk of being a paranoiac. He was blacklisted, he lost his audience, he lost his job, he lost his money. Ten years later they bring him back from a farm in Texas and say, "Gee, yours is an interesting story—you lost everything and you weren't guilty." Guess who brought him back? The media. The people who did that to him. I feel sorry for him, but I can't live the way he did and does.

You can't bring me back. I never left. If you want to pronounce sentence, make it a death sentence. Then you can't feel good about saying, "We're real broad-minded. Ten years later we will bring you on a talk show and say, 'Gee, this is only possible in America.'"

Why do I talk about agents and producers? Are they important in the grand roll of the history of the American republic? Of course not. But they are important to my story because they were the means by which I reached, or was denied, an audience. I wish I had had worthier opponents. I would rather talk about William Colby than about Milt Ebbins. I would rather have talked to J. Edgar Hoover than to Peter Lawford. But I guess I just didn't measure up.

I did have two audiences left to me during this period. One was Las Vegas, the other was the college campuses. I suppose if you are Marshall McLuhan or Jacques Ellul you could read something intriguingly profound into this. Come to think about it, I can. I got to an audience at the Las Vegas Hilton—a middle-class, Gentile audience— through the effort of the late Harvey Orkin, who was a writer who understood the commonality between me and those people who come to Las Vegas, and who are no different from me in their expecting America to be better than it is right now.

Remember Riesman's theory in the 1940's and '50's about people who are inner-directed and other-directed? Well, those Las Vegas audiences and I are both other-directed by Jefferson, Madison, Lincoln, Roosevelt, and Kennedy. We keep believing there is more.

As for the college audiences, they listened to me in the early '50's because they were surprised that a comedian could have written term papers and wondered about the meaning of life in bull sessions. They listened to me in the late '50's and early '60's because they thought I was Beat. They listened to me in the mid-'70's, I think, because I am part of the coinage of their education. When I made fun of Eisenhower, the college audiences thought that I was making chaos out of order. Twenty years later the college audiences are asking me to bring order to chaos: Tell me what it means, man.

Why am I concerned about access to the mass audiences? I am concerned because there isn't any political humor today. And without political humor there isn't any real opposition. If there is any pattern evident in the battlefield of the assassinations, it is that we have never had adversary procedure. Woody Allen is funny, but he is dated. *Love and Death* is Dostoevsky and Tolstoy made Yiddish, which is not to say Jewish.

Nobody's trying to deal with the real black humor of our time. Can you go on national television and describe the trial in Memphis? A man named James Earl Ray shoots Martin Luther King, Jr., drives away in a white Mustang convertible, the least noticeable car available. He is apprehended, returned to the bar of justice. In the courtroom he notifies his attorney, Percy Forman, who comes highly recommended for his success in defending Jack Ruby, that he intends to plead innocent. Forman says the judge will be angry if you do that. How else can he be merciful if you don't plead guilty? The prosecutor, Tennessee Deputy Attorney Philip Canale, rises and says in effect to the court: Your Honor, the State feels it would be in the interests of justice not to have a trial. The defense, apparently in the interests of unity, agrees. The judge, in the interests of mercy, sentences Ray to ninety-nine years.

Or take Clay Shaw in New Orleans. Three judges (under Louisiana's Napoleonic Code) heard the preliminary hearing. Shaw's attorney based his innocence on a lack of evidence against his client as well as on the Warren Report. To dramatize his position, the attorney waved into the courtroom two men with wheelbarrows containing the twenty-six volumes of the Warren Report. As they proceeded down the aisle toward the bench, the three judges conferred with each other. They stated that they would not accept the Warren Report as evidence, since it constituted only hearsay evidence. They then ruled that there was probable cause to bind him over for trial. And the two men with wheelbarrows reached the bench in time to make a U-turn and go back out through the swinging doors.

Now this ought to be the stuff of political humor. But it isn't. Nobody's laughing. I am not laughing either, but that's not the point. I haven't been given all the chances I will someday find to tell the jokes. The terrible, awesome jokes of our time. We are talking here about opportunity. God knows, I've got motive.

People have a choice. You must care how you choose. What will they say that you did? Now, I've come from an America that was divided into some people who believed me and some people who disbelieved me because they were frightened. Perhaps they were paralyzed because they were convinced. First of all, don't stop reading, but consider the source. When you read about history, and when you were present, you are an eyewitness. Don't let somebody with the advantage of distance tell you what happened to you when you were an eyewitness. You were there.

This is a country conceived by Thomas Jefferson, the only country in the Western world that can have a violent change without violent overthrow. How could it break down in fifteen years? Only by plan. Our youth could not go to hell and back. It's not an excursion, this trip to purgatory. Our institutions could not break down. We could not run out of leaders. We could not lose the right to vote. And remember that every time things got good and quiet, either General Wheeler went to Vietnam to get them stirred up again, or Mr. Kissinger went to the Middle East, or an agent provocateur came to your town —whether it was Tommy the Traveler at the State University of New York, or the fella at the University of Michigan who worked for the FBI, or the police sergeant who climbed the flagpole in Grant Park in Chicago and hoisted the Viet Cong flag. But that doesn't mean you've lost your virginity.

Once I was on *The Barry Gray Show* in New York with Abbie Hoffman and his lawyer Gerald Lefcourt, who defended the thirteen Panthers in New York; and Abbie Hoffman said, let's talk about the system being rotten; and Barry Gray asked, how can we make it better? Abbie said, you can't save the system, you have to burn it down. And I said, aren't the terms of your bail in Chicago not to make seditious remarks? I mean, doesn't this endanger your freedom? He said, I don't know about any rules of sedition. I said, I'm not a lawyer but Mr. Lefcourt is, and he isn't cautioning you in any way.

And then I asked about the assassination. Abbie said, "who cares?" And I said, "well it's interesting," then went on to say, very selfishly, "If you want to bring the *Titanic* down, the Ship of State, America, I would think you would exploit Jim Garrison, the District Attorney in New Orleans, whether you like him or not, because he has accused the government of massive crimes. Yet you don't want to join arms with him." "Well," somebody said, "a lot of people died in Vietnam and Jack Kennedy's just another guy." I said, "No, he wasn't. When he was killed, it was a license to kill everybody." By that time the panel sounded like this: "I'm interested in all abuses and how many blacks have been brutalized in this country, not a millionaire from Boston."

It seemed very curious to me. It seemed to me that they were doing what most people were doing. It never is free speech. Abbie Hoffman doesn't open schools to speak in: he writes four-letter words on the wall, he lights up joints of marijuana, and his speaking engagements cancel the entire program for the semester. It was almost as if that were his job.

Let's look at some others. Angela Davis. Angela Davis is a brilliant Ph.D., a very attractive woman, and she chooses to express her anger with the system by joining the Communist Party, which is made up of 850 eighty-six-year-old Jewish people in the Lower East Side of New York and about a thousand FBI agents. Why would she choose such an outmoded form? There's always a trial, a lot of noise, and always there's an acquittal, you'll notice. None of them is ever punished. Then she goes on a speaking tour where the action is—Bulgaria.

Stokely Carmichael couldn't wait to tear the system down; then he was suddenly silent. The man who arrested Dr. Spock and the Reverend William Sloan Coffin, Ramsey Clark, went to Hanoi and suddenly became an outspoken dissident. Daniel Ellsberg, who worked at the Rand Corporation, a CIA-funded group, was in and out of the Marine Corps for thirteen years and suddenly arrived and said he's been redeemed and accused the Army of ruling the country. The Army. Not the CIA. The Army. Who does the CIA speak for? The American financial establishment. And where did Ellsberg speak? He spoke in the New York *Times,* which is more of a financial tribunal that the *Wall Street Journal,* if the truth were known, or if the papers were read from cover to cover. Ellsberg was immediately accepted by the liberals, who don't ever ask for credentials. The left is lovely: You say to them, "I'm turning you in," and they say, "Will you ride to the station with me?"

Ellsberg was immediately accepted because the liberals were starved for heroes, obviously. He went on to discredit the Army, and the concert goes on in the *Times,* an orchestrated scenario. Officers' enlistments are down; the soldiers smoke dope; officers are being fragged by their subordinates. A discreditation of the Army. At the same time, coincidentally, General Abrams caught the Green Berets working for the CIA, killing a double agent and dropping his body in a mail sack in a river in Vietnam, and he said, I don't want any SS in my Army; at which time the CIA said, we're going to drop a real octopus on you, which was My Lai.

When the Warren Report was printed in the New York *Times,* it was printed in one day and buried. The "Pentagon Papers" were printed piecemeal, day by day, as the group that printed it waited to be stopped by the government. Wasn't it the lawyer for the New York *Times* who said in the Supreme Court hearing, "Why don't you define espionage for us so we don't violate the tenets and make it more restrictive?' And Justice Douglas replied by saying, "I find this a very odd argument

107

for a defense counsel." Defense counsel being Alexander Bikel, who wrote in *Commentary*, an influential Jewish monthly, that anybody who didn't accept the Warren Commission must have corrupt reasons.

But there were a lot of people like that. There were people like A. L. Wirin, of the ACLU, who was reported to have said the demise of Oswald was preferable to a blood bath of all those on the left, as a result of the President's death. Intermediaries told me that I. F. Stone said that anyone who didn't accept the conclusions of the Warren Report was exercising irrational judgment. Carey McWilliams of *The New Republic*, otherwise a rational, progressive man, never interpreted the significance of why one of our Presidents was missing.

We lost our innocence in America when the opposition turned out to be disloyal. The dissidents were never a threat, no matter how much they were at variance with the system, until they were subsidized by it. It was reported that the D.A.'s office in Miami donated the sound system to the Yippies and was in turn reimbursed by the federal government at the 1972 convention. In 1968, in Chicago, the CIA found the most vocal, terrifying people —blacks and Yippies—that they could find, bearded people to scare the middle class and justify soldiers on the street of America. The job of the radicals is to promote domestic discord. Once you see the apparatus of the CIA, once you see it work, it becomes opaque. Wasn't it E. Howard Hunt who falsified State Department cables that would give the impression to the American people that Jack Kennedy assassinated Diem? That would blame the war on him. I think Kennedy tried to end that war and has yet to be thanked properly by American youth; he gave them their lives back, while he gave up his own. You can't give much more.

We claim we believe in compassion, which is an abstract, and when it's personified we discredit the man. We say we don't know what kind of President he would have been because he didn't live long enough for us to discover. I know what kind of President he was. I was around for that entire thousand days. I'm an American. I'm involved. I lived in this country. Isn't that enough? You see, when I alerted the American poeple to this military takeover of the government, if you will, I wanted to say, "Remember Miss Liberty, who sent you through school, who gave you birth, who gave you your dreams, who gave you your civility. Don't you owe her something? She is very ill." I never dreamed they would be moved not to her bedside but to her graveside.

The mistake the left always made was that it felt if material was not suppressed by the Hearst newspapers, or whoever the boogeyman was at that time, if they got the facts to the people, the people would rise in righteous indignation. People do not act on information. The distance between taking social action and having the knowledge is as wide as the mouth of the Mississippi. The Gallup Poll reported that when Garrison and I finished after a four-year campaign, there weren't 9 percent of the American people who believed the Warren Report. But they didn't want to do anything about it. It meant overthrowing their lords and masters. What does that mean? It means arresting the members of the Warren Commission and trying them as accessories after the fact. And they won't do it. And they'll die if they don't do it. I would say that's too great a price to pay. Idealistic, cowardly, or whatever you are, it's too great a price. I don't think fascism is worth dying for.

First of all, it'll never work. The most spectacular and successful fascist was Hitler. He had fewer years killing fifty-four million people in World War II than Roosevelt had in free elections. There should be some lesson there.

But how can you live in a country structured by Jefferson and not be impressed? But, of course, the game plan of the CIA is that you won't be impressed. Fascism goes after capitalism; it doesn't bother with communism—that's a duck blind. Whether you're doing that or you're ostensibly several fathoms away, or you're taking the evidence of Watergate and saying, "Well, the overwhelming evidence is that constitutional democracy doesn't work," don't you see that's cynicism? That feeling of hopelessness only serves your masters. It means that you'll be a more pliable public, you won't work for a candidate, and you'll feel negative about everything. I see apparatus working. What is worse, I see it growing. And all these dissidents I've talked about have one thing in common. These people have money. They don't work, they have no means of income, yet they hire lawyers and they fly—they go to Sweden to interview deserters, and they put on demonstrations in cities.

Mike Royko of the *Daily News* in Chicago asked me if there was any blacklisting of me. I said, "What makes you think so?" He said, "Well, everybody who imitates you is prosperous. You're the originator, but you can't get national coverage." I ran into Woody Allen, who once said I was his patron saint. He sat at my feet at the Copacabana one night in 1959 and asked me how to get into show business. Years later I asked him if he was aware of why I wasn't more active and he said, "You can find work —you can always write a book about the assassination." I should have beat the hell out of him, but it looks like somebody did already.

When people did see me work, they would say to me, "Are you all right now?"—as though I'd come back from a mental institution. Yet I took every job offered me. I went to New York, where there was a radio call-in program at NBC called *The Brad Crandall Show*. Brad went on vacation and asked me to fill in for him. I tripled his listenership in four days; I doubled his sponsorship. There was no producer on the program, which meant that no one screened the calls: the discussions consisted of whatever people introduced as subject matter. People called me about the Kennedy assassination, and I answered them. The station called me in and said, "Don't mention Kennedy's name on the air." I said, "How do you keep that out of American history?" They said, "Well, you're a pro."

I was on the air the last night and I had in the booth, among other visitors, Burt Lancaster. The show neared the end, and I was talking about Kennedy's death. A woman called and said, "You evoke such guilt, what do you want us to do? I have a shrine to him over my mantle, a picture of Jack Kennedy and two candles. I light them every time it's his birthday. What do you want me to do?" It was one minute to twelve, I was about to sign off, so I said, "You know what I want you to do? I want you to blow out the candle and curse the darkness." Afterward, at dinner, Lancaster said to me, "Boy, our liberal tendency has sure been exploited. Been led down a primrose path by those Roosevelts and Kennedys." This is a guy who was an acrobat with the Federal Theater in the 1930's. I began to talk to him about the blacklist. He said to me, "There's no blacklist. If you sell tickets, they gotta use you."

Jerry Lewis told me at dinner one night, "The reason you're not working is because you do the news. We've got Chet Huntley, so we don't need you." Then we talked for a while and he said, "Have you ever worked in Vegas?" "Yeah," I said. "Well, you ought to work there again." So he picked up the phone and called Jack Entratter at the Sands, after saying to me, "Remember now, you gotta change your act."

I opened the show for Patti Page, and proved what I always knew: people were dissatisfied with Lyndon John-

111

son and they'd laugh. Not just Beverly Hills Jewish people, but the American people. It went swimmingly. Ed Sullivan was in the audience and he booked me. *Variety* gave me a great review. Metromedia New York called me. Would I like to do a local show in New York?

I went to New York, but I did the Sullivan show first. I walked in and Sullivan said, "Do what you did in Vegas." I did it. I opened up by starting with, "Lyndon Johnson . . . " and Sullivan said, "Hey, hold on, what's this?" I said, "It's the story about my meeting Johnson." Sullivan said, "You never met Johnson." I said, "As a matter of fact, I did." "That's *not* what you did in Vegas." "Yes, it is." "Well, I don't think people want to hear about your meeting a President. It's not believable." Oh, well. I went a little farther and he said, "Why can't you talk about things that are funny . . . like that great comedian . . . his name doesn't come to mind . . . the little red-headed guy." I said, "Woody Allen." "Yeah. Why can't you do what he does?" So I said, "Why didn't you hire him?" "Well, I told you I'd use you, and I keep my word. Now, do what you did in Vegas." "This *is* what I did in Vegas!" I knew he was trying to provoke me to get me to quit. So I didn't say anything. I started again, and I'd get one syllable out of my mouth and he'd sit there like he was pulling the wings off a fly. "You can't say that, you can't say that. That's bigoted, that's narrow-minded, that's *right wing*." I was at this point using only single words, like "Humphrey . . . " Sullivan finally said, "Why don't you come and see me in my office tomorrow at ten o'clock?" I went back to the studio the next day and ran into Jackie Leonard. I asked him, "What are you here for?" "I'm replacing somebody."

Larry Frailberg, the program director at Metromedia New York, decided to call the show, after much deliberation, *Mort Sahl's People*. It was a talk show, of course. I think he copyrighted the title. We settled down to the agony of trying to select guests. The station wanted to put on tough people like Lucille Ball, people who wrote books. I wanted to do a tough show. So, the first week I had on John Chancellor, who had just been appointed head of the Voice of America; and Hefner, who was not shopworn at that time; and Judge Joe Brown, who presided at the trial of Jack Ruby in Dallas; and, at the last moment, I found out that the FBI had been rousting any broadcaster who wanted to have Miriam and Walter Schneir on the air. They had written *Invitation to an Inquest*, which established that the FBI perjured itself in the Rosenberg case. So I had them on. The assassination piece was tremendously revealing, because I ran the film of Ruby shooting Oswald and then I cut to Judge Brown. The show really took off.

The following week there were nothing but meetings and Frailberg told me all his favorites he wanted on the show in the future. The station started to tell me what guests to book. We argued all week. As we got closer to air, we had no guests. Then the station told me, "You will have so-and-so or you will be fired." So, who were the guests they chose? James Farmer, establishment black leader; Mrs. Malcolm X; Dore Schary, to talk about anti-Semitism in Russia; and Cleveland Amory, to talk about cruelty to animals in bullfighting. I figured the only thing I could do was go on the air with this. Because I was being squeezed, because I was being forced out, I figured there was one thing they could not stop. I walked out to the audience *before* the show and told them what was in the wind. The station had recruited an editor of the *National Review* and some professional dissidents to heckle James Farmer. We had a rabbi in the audience and a guy from the American Nazi Party—Hertz rent-a-controversy. I told the audience this. I figured they ought to have an even shot going in. They should be told of this conspiracy against an intellect. In the audience was Metromedia's man Bennett Korn and his date, Joan Fontaine, and some of my fans. So I said, "James Farmer is going to be attacked. He doesn't know it. It's a setup and it's supposed to pass for controversy . . . but it isn't." The station pulled the show and replaced me with wrestling. Gave no reason.

Tom Ryan, a lawyer I met through Herb Sargent, advised me to start action, with the help of the American Federation of Radio and Television Artists, for settlement of my contract with Metromedia. When I got back to Los Angeles, Metromedia called me there, somewhat spontaneously, and said, "We'd like to do a show with you here." I went in to talk about it. The offer came out of left field. They said there was certainly no correlation between the offer and the fact that I was suing them in New York. But they never offered me a show before. I met with Jim Gates, the program director, and I agreed to do the show with them.

The show in L.A. came on with everything moving fast. I mean, the audience was ready. I opened the show with a soliloquy, "Where Have I Been?" and told them about the blacklist.

Rogers and Cowan advised their clients not to be guests on the program. When I wanted to bring certain actors on, they were told to keep away. Richard Harris was one of these. When I met him he told me, "I'm an Irish rebel; I'll be on." The night he was to appear, he called me fifteen minutes before air time to say that he had been taken to a hospital because he had suddenly become ill. He later remarked that Jack Riley—Harris did not know that Riley worked for me on the show—said to him, "You ought to get together with Mort sometime." Harris said, "I'm not sure he likes me. Might've resented what I did to him." I asked Newman to be on the program and he never answered me.

Budd Schulberg hated the program because we did a takeoff of his "Angry Voices of Watts," his black writers' workshop. Ours was called "The Angry Voices of Beverly Hills." We showed all the frustrated people meeting at La Scala to have their writers' workshops and express themselves and shed some of their frustrations. We had a producer's wife who read her poem:

> *I'm looking for a man.*
> *Any kinda man.*
> *I don't care whether he works*
> *For his father or my father,*
> *As long as he's a man.*

The Kennedy assassination information grew on the KTTV program to where it was a department. One week, the station fired me. No notice. The station had five thousand pickets by nightfall. They received thirty-one thousand letters from the L.A. area in three days. I then got a call from Chuck Young, the station manager. He just happened to have a film crew from the nightly news waiting in the hall, so he could get an announcement on the six o'clock news that I'd be back on the air the following night. When I opened the show, the first shot was a physical re-creation of *Mr. Smith Goes to Washington.* I stood in front of a table (much like Jimmy Stewart in the Senate) overflowing with telegrams and letters, and I couldn't be heard above the applause for twelve minutes.

It's a curious thing. The Channel 11 execs didn't want me to go on attacking the Warren Report. They said, "That's point of view," which is not allowed to individuals, let alone television personalities.

One day in 1966 my wife, China, and I were reading and listening to television and heard a news bulletin: "A New Orleans lawyer claims to have unearthed evidence of a conspiracy to assassinate President Kennedy. The D.A.'s office says arrests will be made shortly." China said, "That's not a lawyer. It's Jim Garrison. He's the D.A." By this time the reporter was attacking Garrison's credentials. I asked China, "Is he corrupt?" "No," she said. "I've known him ten years. He's incorruptible." Channel 11 sent me down to New Orleans to see if I could get an interview. The result was that I did the first national interview with Garrison, which was ninety minutes long.

Arriving in New Orleans, I got into a cab and said to the cabbie, "4600 Owens Boulevard." "That's Jim Garrison's house! I'll let you off on the corner. I don't want to get shot. Somebody says there's a machine gun pointed at his door." "What do you think of this thing Garrison's got?" The driver said, "I believe those bastards in Washington are capable of anything—and a lot worse."

I walked to the door and a man emerged, all six foot seven inches of him, wearing a bathrobe. I said, "I'm Mort Sahl, and I came down here to shake your hand." Garrison said, "I hope you're available to do a lot more than that." Later, he took me into a wine cellar at the Royal Orleans Hotel and opened up the Manila envelope that was the beginning of a compilation of a four-year investigation. It contained documents on Pentagon and Central Intelligence Agency involvement in the events surrounding the Kennedy assassination.

Who was involved? I recall at a press conference that Garrison spoke of "the right wing," and a reporter said, "But you've also charged the CIA and others." Garrison's reply still holds. "These are not mutually exclusive groups. Usually a conspiracy involves more than one person."

That was the first time that I knew more than I would like to know. Yet, you can't know less than you know. I wanted to work for Garrison, so I got my credentials and a desk in the D.A.'s office, took an apartment in New Orleans, and went out to do college concerts when I needed money to buy groceries and pay the rent.

Later, I went to New York and onto *The Tonight Show*. I met with Rudy Tellez, the producer, and said to him, "Rudy, I don't want to throw you any curves. What's *verboten* on this show?" I've always done that, although the networks like a characterize me as an outlaw, because it justifies capital punishment. Rudy said, "Don't mention Sarnoff. It's the only 'No.'" I said, "Even if I talk about the Warren Commission, it's OK?" "Yes, if you don't editorialize and you read it straight." So I agreed. We went on the air that night. I was on the panel and Carson said to me, "What're you doing now?" I told him I lived in New Orleans part of the time. When I mentioned that I knew Garrison, Carson started to laugh. He said, "You don't put any faith in that, do you?" And I answered, "Yes, I put every faith in it. He's the most important man in America." Carson said, "Look at what the press said and everything." I told him that the press was doctored. That they wanted to stop him. "*Why* do they want to stop him?" I continued. "Because he has the truth. There has been a great suppression of the truth in this case. If he's a crackpot, why not let him expose himself?" Carson said, "One week from tonight." "You've got it," I said. We went off the air. Carson's chest was swelled; he was so happy to give people their rights, piecemeal. Off the air, Carson said, "Listen, I don't want this thing to become a circus."

David Merrick—he looks like the leading man in a dirty movie—had been on the program and he said, "Yeah, we don't want to give a crackpot a lot of publicity." And Stan Irwin said, "Yeah, we don't want to give this guy a lot of mileage." I talked them all out of canceling

117

the promised show and took off for New Orleans that night. I got Garrison and told him we'd start rehearsing. "I'll make up three-by-five index cards. I'll play Carson and you be you." ("Oh," Carson had said to me, "we'll have to have someone on from the government, to give equal time. The network is very good on equal time.")

You may recall that one of the two missing persons in the Clay Shaw trial was Gordon Novell, a former CIA agent. He was one of the equal-timers. The men who wrote the white papers against Garrison—NBC produced two of them—called the first one "The Trial of Jim Garrison." Apparently, they forgot who killed the President. The researchers were headed by Walter Sheridan, who had been a Justice Department lawyer hot after Hoffa, under Bobby Kennedy's direction. For him to have become a newsman, as Bill Stout at CBS told me, was pretty odd—"Pretty odd for NBC to bring in a house detective and call him a reporter." Odd, indeed.

When Gordon Novell fled New Orleans, two girls who had rented his apartment discovered a note imbedded under a panel in which Novell indicated his intention to return to the CIA, which he felt was his destiny anyway.

I started to brief Garrison for the Carson show. He asked me, "Who do you think they'll have on from the Warren Commission?" I said nobody. I said that because I was on the air in California for fifty-eight weeks talking about the Kennedy assassination and had offered the air to the Warren Commission members and counsel. Nobody took me up on it. Anybody who has read the whole Warren Report cannot defend it. So I said, "You watch and see if they don't call and say there will be nobody." I rehearsed with Garrison one whole week, and when he went on the air, I had foreseen every question Carson would ask except one. The day before air, I heard from Carson. "Who's going to debate Jim?" I asked him. "I will," he said. "I holed up one Saturday afternoon and read the Warren Report." That is interesting, because it took me twenty-seven months to read the Report.

Garrison went to New York. Ironically, the man who was thought to be a big threat to the system upped Carson's audience from nine million to fourteen million—the highest rating he'd ever had. Garrison did the entire ninety minutes alone. Carson interrupted Garrison seventeen times in the first twenty-five minutes. Garrison produced a photograph of eleven men being caught by the Dallas Police, arrested and handcuffed, in the freight yards. And Garrison asked Carson to identify the "lone assassin." Johnny replied that his cameras could not pick up glossies. At one point Carson asked, "Jim, why would Lyndon Johnson cover this up?" Garrison said, "I don't know why, Johnny; why don't you ask him?" The audience warmed to Garrison. The next day in New Orleans, Garrison received two thousand telegrams by nine in the morning from various D.A.s around the country. People were impressed by Carson's nervous antagonism and in effect said, "Garrison must have something, judging from the way he was continually interrupted."

It became so bad that NBC sent out thousands of form letters saying that the Johnny seen on TV that night was not the Johnny we all know and love—that he had to play the devil's advocate because that makes for a better program. When they apologized for him, Carson became furious and said that Garrison would never be on the air again and *I* would never be on the air again.

In time Garrison and Executive Assistant D.A. Andy Sciambra and I fell into black humor as we pursued this case. For instance, I was eventually fired by Channel 11 ostensibly because, while they would not censor me, they insisted I have new evidence if I persisted with the assassination story. I went on the air one week and said that Oswald, Ruby, and Shaw had met at the Capitol Hotel in Baton Rouge. I was fired. The program had an even rating with the Carson show in the Los Angeles area. It became evident to me what kind of power we were playing with.

I returned to New Orleans. Garrison had charged Dean Andrews, who had been Lee Harvey Oswald's lawyer. He had been visited in his office by Oswald and an unidentified pair of Cuban men, one described as thick-necked. Andrews said he had been contacted by Marguerite Oswald, Lee's mother, about defending him. He later retracted this and said it had happened while he was in the hospital and he was under sedation and he might have been dreaming, Andrews was charged with perjury in connection with his testimony before the Grand Jury, where he said that Clay Bertrand and Clay Shaw were not the same man. Off the record, he said that if he talked, those in Washington would put a hole in his head. When Andrews was sentenced on the perjury charge, Garrison worried that Andrews' heart condition would be aggravated by confinement in prison. So when Andrews appealed his conviction to the Supreme Court, the District Attorney signed the appeal. He did not serve time.

Then we subpoenaed Marina Oswald. I recall she was walking down the street with her new husband, Mr. Porter, who looked not so much like a husband as he did a Secret Service man following, or escorting, her. She got up in the Grand Jury room and looked very glassy-eyed. Garrison asked if there were something wrong. Her husband said, "Well, she was raised in Soviet Russia and that's a totalitarian country." Garrison said, "Well, if she's had a rehearsal she should be perfectly acclimated to living in the United States under this administration." (Garrison often referred to Washington as "The Fourth Reich.")

Jim Garrison was in a position to become governor of Louisiana or the next senator. He was the most influential Democrat in Louisiana, and he had political friends in other parts of the South. He blew all that. Nowadays people say that he did what he did for political aggrandizement or that he pursued the Shaw case for political ambition. The fact is that the best way in the world to advance yourself in politics is to *not* attack the federal government. But Jim is an honest man, and he knew no other way to express himself. At the age of fifty-three, Jim Garrison is out of a job, has less than $5,000 in the bank, an ex-wife and five kids to support, a Volkswagen his wife drives, and a lot of seven-year-old shirts from Brooks Brothers. But he has himself, unmortgaged, and that's more than I can say for some of the other people I've listed here.

I noticed that there was nothing contagious about courage. I would go in and out of New York and Los Angeles, and I found that they were burying the President under history—Sorensen and Schlesinger were writing it. They were burying the memory. They were pretending that Cleveland followed Eisenhower. The truth hurts, but the lies will kill you. The price of lying about Jack Kennedy is fifty-six thousand Americans killed in Vietnam, God knows how many Asians; the destruction of the American dollar; and a civil war between the CIA and the Army, which expresses itself through Ellsberg's revelations or James McCord's letter to Judge Sirica. With Nixon's departure we witnessed the second assassination of a President by the CIA in ten years.

In order to get some witnesses in the case against Shaw, we called in a girl named Barbara Reed, who is a sort of Perle Mesta of the French Quarter. She walked into Garrison's office and recognized Sciambra. They had known each other from the Bourbon House, a place in the French

Quarter also frequented by Lee Harvey Oswald and Clay Shaw. She said, accusingly, "Well, you're playing liberal now, but where were you when we wanted a black studies program at school?" Sciambra, who came from an impoverished family, said, "Listen, until I was nineteen, I thought everybody was an Italian." Then Garrison asked me to take Barbara to a party and just listen with two big ears. I said, "Barbara Reed doesn't appeal to me." And Garrison said, deadpan, "For a man who purports to love his country, you certainly won't stand up when I ask you to make a small sacrifice." He reminded me of the courage of Thomas Jefferson.

So I went to the party, where we met another fellow, Layton Martens, whom we charged with perjury. He said to me, "I have nothing against you fellows. You were only doing your job, and I was doing mine."

Shaw's arrest was interesting. Garrison had a witness named Perry Russo, who said he had been at a party at David Ferry's house with Clay Shaw and Lee Harvey Oswald. Shaw on that occasion discussed how one could use a triangulation of fire to murder the President in a car caravan. Russo was the witness to this. Now, we brought Shaw in, and Garrison said to him as he approached his desk, "I charge you with conspiracy to murder John F. Kennedy."

Perspiration broke out on Shaw's upper lip. He said, "I'd like to go home and get some of my things." To Garrison, that meant hide some things. So Garrison wanted to go over and search the house. He said, "I think you'd better go downstairs and be booked and have bail set." When he went downstairs, the desk sergeant said, "Is this your name?" Shaw said, "Sure." "Any aliases?" "Clay Bertrand," Shaw said. "Bertrand" is of course derived from the Marquis de Sade, whose inclinations Shaw was more than casually acquainted with as a life style. During the trial he claimed that he never used the pseudonym Clay Bertrand as the name of the man who hired Dean Andrews to defend Oswald. The significance was that Garrison was certain that Shaw was Bertrand, whereas the "NBC White Paper" group produced a bartender who claimed to use the same name.

The D.A.'s investigators went to Shaw's apartment while he was being booked. They found a black hood, an executioner's whip, and wooden shoes, which Shaw said he used for the Mardi Gras—curious, since the shoes had obviously never touched anything but a rug. So they went to trial. Shaw was acquitted because he said he didn't know Oswald, although Fred Liemans, the proprietor of a steam bath in New Orleans, said that they used to come to the baths and disappear together for hours at a time. Liemans was approached by a government agency which urged him not to continue to give state's evidence. It sounded, from his story, like the Internal Revenue Service.

I announced this on *The Dick Cavett Show*. I was followed out of the studio by two Internal Revenue agents. I said to them at 51st and Madison, "Why don't we stop playing the game. I'm not bound by law to talk to you without an attorney." They replied "We want to know the name of the agent who abused his power by threatening an audit." I asked, "Why don't you call your field office and find out?" They said, "We're not supposed to make long-distance phone calls." I asked if the government was on a budget. They asked if Garrison had actually heard the threat to Liemans. I told them to call Garrison. The agents answered that they felt Garrison probably wouldn't take their call. I said, "Well, fellows, the charade is over. I believe that the government killed the President, and you work for the government. So what are we talking about?" One of the agents said, "Oh, come on, Mort, we're not CIA; we're Treasury."

It's hard to telescope a four-year investigation. Perry Russo, our first witness, then had a visit from Walter Sheridan of the Justice Department. We had planted a recorder on Russo, and he recorded Sheridan's offering him an alternative to testifying against Shaw. It was a job in Los Angeles, which Sheridan assured Russo was outside Garrison's jurisdiction. Which, of course, is what they did with a witness against Garrison's subsequent punitive trials. Pershing Gervais was sent to Vancouver by the government, given a job at $40,000 a year, and a new identity. It has been rumored that the only reason Gervais blew the whistle was that when the government took out withholding, he became disenchanted. He expected his pay to be clear of taxes and Social Security. Garrison has since been acquitted, something like six times, on all these charges.

Perry Russo, we feel, backed off because he was being blackmailed and was fearful for his future. Russo's is an amazing case. During the trial, Mr. Diamond, one of Shaw's mighty legal eagles, said to him, "Did you hear them say at the party they were going to kill the President?" Russo said, "Yes." "Well, it was a party," Diamond continued. "Couldn't they have been joking?" You know, you go to a party, and there's salted peanuts and vodka and tonic, and a lot of loose talk, and somebody can even joke about how to murder the President.

The final day of the Shaw trial, the last witness was Colonel Pierre Finck of the Army Medical Corps, who apparently came down to testify because he felt there might be a miscarriage of justice if he did not intercede on Clay Shaw's behalf. Which would mean, if it's true, that he was somewhat prejudiced as a witness. But Garrison's assistant, Al Oser, was a fair guy. He let him on anyway and asked him, "Colonel, did you do the autopsy?" The Colonel said, "Yes, I did." Oser asked Finck if he had sectioned the President's head. Finck hadn't. Oser asked if he had traced the path of the wounds. Finck hadn't. Garrison asked if he had turned the President over to look at his back. Finck hadn't. He said they had looked at his back in Texas. Oser asked Finck why he had not done any of these things. Finck said that a Major General from the Pentagon was standing at the President's head, and told him he was running the show. No matter how obscure the people Garrison charged, lawyers endowed with national reputation and undeniable ability rose to the occasion. Who subsidized them remained a mystery to me.

In an effort to recruit some muscle for Garrison, because I was probably the only well-known name on his side, I went to Washington and spoke with Gene McCarthy. "What about the trial?" McCarthy said. "There wasn't only one conspiracy against Jack. There were four. But nobody wants to deal with it. And I think when Garrison gets to bat, they'll characterize him as a madman, and the press will help." He was right.

Then I went to see George McGovern. He has Jack's old office. I asked him what he thought about the case. McGovern said, "Well, I think the Warren Report is a lot of crap." I asked him what he thought we could do. McGovern said, "I think it's up to the family to investigate his murder." I said, "You know, grieving is a private affair, but murder is a public affair, Senator. And besides, what family? They're all dead. I mean, if President Johnson were to be shot, God forbid, must we rely on his brother to investigate it?" So McGovern said to me, "Well, he wasn't that good a President, anyway." I said, "Is that punishable by death?" That was the last time I saw George McGovern for some time. Until he emerged playing tapes during the convention to illustrate how close he was to the Kennedys.

The pressure took other forms. In Chicago, Kupcinet,

the most influential columnist, who had been a friend of mine, said to me, "You know, I know Jack Ruby, and he couldn't be capable of what you say." That's the old theory the liberals have, you know, that Oswald couldn't have worked for the government because he was dumb. You see, the government never hires dumb people. Enrico told me Kup had asked him if I still talked that much about the assassination. After a show in Chicago, when I finally had found a way to make the audience not only look at the Warren Report but laugh at it, he said to me that I should stop mentioning that—it was indecent. It's the first time I heard that a columnist tried to edit me. Certainly nightclub owners don't.

There's always the question of where you are, and where you ought to be. You remember the movies. You remember the endings. The cowboy, having restored order to the town, looks down on the rancher and his daughter. The rancher says, "Stranger, I wish you'd change your mind and settle down here." The cowboy, who has the horizon behind and in front of him, says, "No, thank you kindly. But I've gotta ride on." Well, I've been trying to ride out of New Orleans for ten years. New Orleans is the most important city in America in the last hundred years. It's where Oswald was bred, where he worked for Guy Bannister and Naval Intelligence, where Donald Ferry was, where Clay Shaw was, where Gordon Novell was, where the command post was. It was where Victor Marchetti first reported that he heard Richard Helms express concern over Garrison's upcoming prosecution of Clay Shaw. It was where William Colby, addressing a convention, said that he could not deny that Shaw was a CIA agent. It was where Senator Schweiker promised to focus future investigations directly on the New Orleans area and where the lawmaker pointed out that Lee Harvey Oswald had contact with anti-Castro Cuban groups. And it was there that the District Attorney made the initial, and what was to be the only, thrust to seek justice for *the* fallen President. Even the Senate Intelligence Committee agrees on the significance of New Orleans in the plans to murder President Kennedy.

The knowledge that great crimes can go unmentioned, even go unpunished, just the stupidity of it, is more damaging to the idea of Jefferson's Republic than malice. The effect of CIA activity, the promotion of domestic discord, is shattering upon a country that somehow tied itself together for a hundred and eighty years. People became not Americans, but one nation highly divisible. They became Indians, Blacks, Women, Chicanos.

Mark Lane attacks the Warren Commission by saying in *Rush to Judgment* that the Commission didn't name the perpetrators, but he stops short of determining who they would be. Well, I don't know how anybody could have any theory except one, which becomes evident: that the CIA and the Pentagon murdered the President. It's quite obvious from the people who are in the case, the material witnesses, and from the aims of those involved. You just look at those who benefitted from that assassination, and you work somewhat backward.

Mark Lane was on my program five times in Los Angeles, establishing his credentials as a fearless investigator, the master of dissent. He got a great deal of publicity, and he sold a lot of books. When he wrote his second book, he referred to me with great gratitude by saying that he had been on my program. Actually, it was a little more than that: I had been fired as a result of having him on five times, and I had been fired from radio for having him on my radio program. It was the highest-rated nighttime radio program in the city of Los Angeles. Mr. Lane then acted as my attorney just long enough to advise me to quit a Broadway show, and when I asked for further legal advice after I was sued, he was remarkably unavailable. Sciambra used to say if Dracula tried to drive a stake through his heart, he'd be in real trouble: the myth would be over.

Lane went to California and joined forces with Jane Fonda to protest the Vietnam War. When the Kennedy assassination turned out not to be a radical cause, he moved on, and spoke on campuses against the war, grew a beard, wore an Army field jacket, opened up GI coffeehouses with posters of Bob Dylan and Joan Baez in them.

One night, after not seeing him for four or five years, he knocked on my door at three in the morning. He walked in with Donald Sutherland and Jane Fonda. I'd received a call earlier in the day from Garrison, who told me that they'd been in New Orleans to see him. The three told him that they were going to make a movie about the assassination, and Garrison said to them that I was the guy to see about the film. He told them I had to participate in the movie because I "overlapped." I knew the rules of evidence, and I was also in the arts. But when they came to my house, they foolishly assumed that I hadn't talked to Garrison.

Jane asked me, "If you were going to do a movie about the assassination, how would you do it?" I asked if they were going to do such a movie. They all said no. I proceeded to tell them that the way I would have done it some years ago was definitely not the same way I would do it now, because we're somewhat separated by time from the shock of November 1963. But I told them I would make it abstract, or, at any rate, not specifically the Kennedy case. I would have a reporter, a skeptical reporter, a very cynical guy, together with a girl reporter investigating the case. Neither of them would believe in conspiracy, but the conspiracy would eventually kill the girl. The man would then feel a sense of loss and would understand the horror of murder. Before I finished the last word of the plot, Jane Fonda said the idea stank. I said, "It's not too bad a scenario for the money." Nobody laughed. We talked a little bit and somebody said something about ruthlessness. I said that Jim Garrison was relentless but not ruthless. Donald Sutherland said, "I don't see why you can't combine both," and then made some speech about Guevara. He was sullen.

At that point my wife, China, said to Mark, "Why did you walk away and let Mort drown in a lawsuit, and how can you walk in here three years later?" He said, "Oh, I wanted to know how he is." China said, "It can't be very urgent if it held for three or four years. I don't want you in my house. Just get out." I explained to Fonda and Sutherland that the situation was embarrassing, but it involved only Mark and China and me. I apologized to them because they were in the middle of it. They left.

All the things that caused Garrison and me to be labeled paranoids came to be true. We saw that the CIA does train local police departments. We saw that the federal government is not to be trusted. We saw that government officials do tap telephones. We saw that they do take bribes. We saw that the CIA does start wars, implicating the Army, and that the Army in turn implicates the people. After we said these things, no one said you guys were right. No, instead they said that "you embarrass us. We can forgive you for what you said, but we can't forgive you for being right." Believe me, actual sin is a lot tougher to take than original sin. It was busy in New Orleans. The Black Panthers had barricaded themselves in a housing project and said they would die in a suicide mission for equal housing. They didn't live there obviously, because no tenant would ever defend those apartments with such fervor. In keeping with the unique color of New Orleans, the project was named "Desire."

In case the Indians at Wounded Knee were too remote to be a threat, a Navy yeoman arrived on the roof of Howard Johnson's in New Orleans and turned out to be a good enough marksman to take just about everybody out. There was total anarchy except, as usual, some official finds the explanatory note in the charred ruins which says: "I did it because I hate white folks" or "I did it because I hate capitalism." (Just in case you don't know who your enemies are or you lost your way in some other fashion.) It looked very much like a Company job to keep the issue confused. Suddenly Evans and Novak are down there and Novak is writing how great Mayor Landrieu is, pulling this town together—and all this is prior to Garrison's run for re-election—because the D.A. isn't taking care of law and order. Novak also went on to say (on Los Angeles KHJ Channel 9) that the most damaging thing in this country are people like Mort Sahl, who issue reports that the government killed the President and make charges which only divide us as a nation. The rest of the time Novak has done his best to discredit Eugene McCarthy. But then, McCarthy concludes that the press never wanted a President who was smarter than the press.

There are no anonymous murders anymore. When a computer is blown up, we hear people say, "Well, we found in the charred ruins a sign saying, 'We did it because we hate capitalism. Sincerely yours, the Left.'" They're very smart, the CIA. I've said they're unethical, I've said they're murderers, but you may note I've yet to say they're not professional. Well, what else have they got to do? And they've got all the money in the world to do it with. Our money. To sit there and plan these things, day by day and hour by hour, to come up continually with capers to convince you the system is fallible. And mostly, to choose a position on the left, to staff the left. They don't staff the right—that'll take care of itself; they staff the left. They give a fellow a liberal credential, they'll let you trust him, and they'll always give you a cookie. A guy writes an article for *Ramparts* and says, "The Gulf Oil Company wants to start a war so they can drill offshore in Vietnam." The reader says, "Wow, what revelations." That's your cookie.

I spent years talking with people, Garrison notably, about the Kennedy assassination, and I was said to have hurt my career by being in bad company. I don't think Gene McCarthy is bad company. I don't think that Jack Kennedy is bad company. I don't think that Garrison is bad company. I learned something, though. The people that I went to the Hollywood parties with are not my comrades. The men I was in the trenches with in New Orleans are my comrades. The ones who underwent the ordeal of combat, especially the brave ones who knew we could not win and put that to one side, threw away the blueprint, and went on about the job of construction, knowing that the only definition of life is purpose. I think Jack Kennedy cries from the grave for justice.

After making the first comedy records in America, and after making seven of them, I couldn't make a single record deal. Alan Livingston, who is at Capitol Records, told me if I kidded President Johnson, they'd be sued by him. That would be laughable in itself. But they signed me and thereby paralyzed me for two years—no record was ever made. After starring on network television myself to a point where I had my own special show for Pontiac, I couldn't get on any program. It's been quite a while since any of you have seen me on a network. Yet I did a lot of talk shows. I did *The Tonight Show* and Carson said, "Gee, we don't see you anymore." I suppose that's the worst baiting of all. I think that's what I couldn't believe about America the most. No one rebelled. Because I know myself that if you told me not to hire somebody, I'd make him the vice president of the firm.

What happened to this country as the crucible of rebellion? They had made eunuchs of the men by showing them what they might lose. Freud called it conditioning against failure. They did a pretty thorough job. When I was proposed by a manager for *The Dean Martin Show*, I told them I'd do any material they wanted, which was so unlike me that it should have made them suspicious. I was very tractable. Hal Kemp, the producer, said I wasn't welcome if I sang the "Star Spangled Banner" and read the "Gettysburg Address." This is the man who originally signed me for the National Broadcasting Company in 1956 as a great new find. There was no one to take the issue to. Even when the liberals found that Agnew and Nixon were repugnant to them, no one called on me to satirize either of them. They were afraid to endorse me even by enlisting me against an easy adversary. I was too dangerous to be on staff.

When Brando decided to march to Mississippi, he called me up one night and asked me to dinner. He's the only artist, one of a select few, whom I can separate from his character. I mean, his work is so monumental that I would stand in line to see him. In the past, I'd found him less than civil. For instance, at the time he directed and acted in the movie *One-Eyed Jacks*, all the studios were jockeying and lobbying in the trade papers for awards. I took out an ad in the back of *The Hollywood Reporter* and *Daily Variety* and nominated him as the best director.

I went over to his house and Richard Harris was there. Now, Brando prides himself on being cagey, and he said, "I've got Harris here because I'm suing over *Mutiny on the Bounty*. Harris was in the cast and he can be my witness." In other words, it wasn't just a free dinner. He was going to get that much out of Harris. Then he turned to me and said, "Will you go to Mississippi on Sunday and march for us?" That was one thing about the liberals: they knew that when I march, nobody laughs. Brando said he was going to march for the Negroes in Mississippi. Did I want to go? I said I didn't. He said, "It'll be great publicity." I found that shocking, but I still don't think publicity motivates him.

And then he talked to me about the value of money all evening, and how he was putting money away. Money would insulate him. I said, "If we're going to be candid, I want to tell you something that's a larger problem than being black." I told him I thought I was blacklisted because I kept broadcasting the President's death and the false reports of it. And he said, "Well, screw them." Which I was not in a position to do.

In the interim, while I talked to the people at the party, he went to my girl, China. He said he was well off and taking care of several girls. He asked her what was the nature of our relationship. She said why don't you ask Mort. He finally told me I was a phony liberal because when I was called to the colors, I wouldn't go to Mississippi. But of course the real reason I wouldn't go was because I was ordered to.

One of the torturous aspects of that period was that people would bring up the assassination gratuitously but not seriously. It happened when I was dating the girl I eventually married, China Lee. I met China in San Francisco. We later talked often by phone—I was in New York and she was living in San Francisco. China, as I said earlier, knew Jim Garrison from her home town. One of China's brothers—there are eight children in her family—

took flying lessons from Lee Harvey Oswald in the Civil Air Patrol in New Orleans. In addition to that, Perry Russo, Garrison's chief witness in the trial against Clay Shaw, knew China when she was nine years old and was her childhood next-door boyfriend. In addition to that, Garrison's Executive Assistant D.A., Andy Sciambra, was at Loyola Law School with China's brother Harry, who is now a federal judge. In addition to that, Harry, before being a judge, was legislative assistant to Majority Leader of the House of Representatives Hale Boggs (D. Louisiana).

Now, the Ford Motor Company made a practice of leasing cars to political officials for a dollar a year. Once, when I was in New Orleans, Harry let me use his car. China and I picked up Garrison to take him to dinner. I opened the glove compartment of the car to get something and found the registration slip made out to Hale Boggs, who, of course, was on the Warren Commission. I pointed out to Garrison that I was driving him to dinner in a limousine belonging to a man he was trying to arrest as a member of the Warren Commission!

Although others see China as exotic, I see her as being determined and strong-willed. That's why she's excelled as a swimming champion, as a photographer, and at anything else she attempted. She was raised in a strict Chinese family. I made a mistake in assuming that Chinese are patriarchal, but it turns out they are a lot like the Jews, who honor their fathers and listen to their mothers.

The year I met her, she was in thirteen movies. Later, she didn't do as many because she was associated with me. John Frankenheimer asked China to visit him at MGM to talk about a movie, and all he talked to her about was my concern over the assassination of John Kennedy. At the time, Frankenheimer and I had been close, and he recommended to George Axelrod that I direct his next film. Yet, when my name was brought up later in public, he did what so many people in Hollywood did at that time. He said, "I don't speak to him." These were imagined fights. In Act One, we were friends; in Act Three, I was repugnant; and there was no second act. China did a special with Joey Bishop. The director, Dick Carson (Johnny's brother, who now directs the *Merv Griffin Show*), while not downright unfriendly, fixedly interrogated her about me and the assassination. I don't recall Art Linkletter or John Wayne ever baiting me. Jack Webb is another matter.

I got to know Webb through Bobby Troup, who married Webb's ex-old lady, Julie London. Webb, of course, was famous for doing a show called *Dragnet*, which was written by a guy, a talented drinker, named Dick Breen. In *Pete Kelly's Blues*, Breen is credited for that very funny line by Janet Leigh. She asks her guy, "When can we get married?" He says, "As soon as I get my band together. Just give me a little time." Janet Leigh says, "I don't want to wait so long that when they throw the rice, it knocks me down." The best parts of *Dragnet* were written by Breen. When Breen died, Webb tried to carry on the *Dragnet* formula, which goes something like this:

Webb voice-over (while he is ringing doorbell):
  It's 10:47 A.M.
WEBB: Are you the landlady?
LANDLADY: Yes, I am. Would you officers like
  some coffee?
WEBB: No, ma'am, I'm not married. Now, was
  there anything strange about this roomer?
LANDLADY: No, he was a nice boy. Always kept his
  room clean. Nice boy, nice boy.
WEBB: Well, is there anything else you can
  tell us?

LANDLADY: No, officers. He was a mighty nice
boy—always tidy, and always hung up the
phone in the hall.

WEBB: Thank you, ma'am. We'll be in touch
with you if there is anything else we'd like to
ask you.

LANDLADY: Oh, officers . . . there was *one*
thing. . . .

WEBB: Yes, ma'am, what was that?

LANDLADY: He was a midget.

That was the show.

Anyway, Jack Webb, who never goes out of his house
except to go back and forth to the studio, asked me over
to his house once. It was during the writers' strike at
Universal. (I had marched in the picket line with a sign
that read, "Producers! Please don't rewrite my sign.")
Anyway, we went over to Webb's house. Webb stays in
his rumpus room, which has an eighteen-hundred-watt
high-fidelity system, a hundred and twenty-eight speak-
ers, original Benny Goodman records, records of Gershwin
playing the piano for Fred Astaire, a titanium arm weigh-
ing one gram for his turntable, and sixteen Sony monitors
to pick up every television station.

Webb told me that I could be a writer, because, "You
hear dialogue, and I can make you into a writer. I want
to work with you." I asked him what he would pay for
the scripts. When he gave me the answer, I laughed, because it was what I make in a nightclub in about an hour.
He said he could make me a producer, so I would make
some extra money—I could produce a show about firemen
called *Emergency*. I told him that I didn't think I could
quit my job to take an office at the studio, wear an alpaca
sweater, and go to lunch at Universal Studios, where I was
producing a show about firemen. I asked him, "Why
would I want to do that?" "I tell you why, buddy," Webb

told me. "M-O-N-E-Y." He asked me to give it a try, just to write him something, whatever I felt like writing.

I was working on this book, writing an article for *Playboy*, and a lot of other things. Anyway, I had come across an article in the paper about the killer military dogs in Vietnam. The army was killing them because they could not be retrained to be docile. I wrote about a sergeant leaving Vietnam who goes to his battalion commander and asks him, "Why are you killing these dogs?" The commander says, "Because they are trained for war, not to fit into society." The sergeant says, "Well, by the same token, I could go out and execute my whole platoon." The sergeant takes a dog back with him and uses him in his police patrols.

I took it to Webb and did what I always do with screenplays: I acted it out for Webb and Bob Cinader, a producer, and Jake Shearer, Webb's lawyer. The title of the script was "Alert." Webb thought that was fantastic. I told him we could spin it off from *Adam-12*.

Webb later said that he had a problem: he was not going to do any more cop shows, and he had no place to use my script. But, he wanted to use one of the characters in the script for an existing show. The character? The guard dog! He wanted to use the dog in a show called *Chase*, about four cops. One cop is a mortorcycle rider, one is a helicopter pilot, one is a hot-rodder, and Webb thought that the fourth cop should have a dog—you know, for sniffing out narcotics, etc. They wanted to buy my dog for that show. I said, "You want to license the character, but you don't want the show? What does that involve?" He said, "Well, we'll pay you a royalty." I asked how much. Webb said, "One hundred dollars, when we use him."

I said I had a better idea. I told him it was time I got on television to help my career. I said to him, "Why don't you make me a lieutenant working on *Chase?* I'll be on the show, and I'll give you that story." "We can't do that," Webb said. "There is no room for other characters." Cinader said, "Besides, you can't act." I said, "I've just been signed by Peckinpah for the second lead in *Bring Me the Head of Alfredo Garcia.*" Cinader said "Well, Peckinpah has no talent either."

Later on, I picked up a *TV Guide* and read about *Chase:* "The story about four policemen, one of whom has a dog!" I wrote Webb a letter. The next thing I knew, checks for $100 were coming to me. I never cashed one of them. I had a lawyer get in touch with Webb. Webb wanted to settle, but first he wanted to read me my rights. Universal wanted to settle. The insurance company wanted to settle. I haven't seen Webb since.

One day I saw Rod Serling, and he said, "I saw you on television the other night. And you implied that I was a gasbag, a do-nothing liberal." I said, "You mean a social democrat, in my vernacular." And he said, "Well, I resent that." I said, "How much do you resent? What about the fact that I haven't been able to get a job for four years?" And Serling said, "I never heard about that." I said, "Well, you're hearing it from me." As we parted, Serling said, "You're a good man. We need more like you. Hang in there." Guilt is the check you can't cash.

When I visited Washington, John Chancellor had advanced from the days of covering the Stevenson primaries (when I had met him in 1956): he was in line to take over Chet Huntley's job. He didn't speak of Kennedy, alive or dead. We ate dinner, and as the girls did the dishes, Chancellor walked me out into the garden and he said to me, "Listen. I have an idea for you to get on the road back." This was his admission that I had been derailed. And I said, "What is it?" He said, "Call Dick

Goodwin at the White House [the Johnson White House] and tell him you read his book and you love it." I said, "I didn't read it." He said, "Well, that doesn't matter. He'll be caught up with the compliment and he won't check." I said, "What will that mean?" He said, "Well, once you know Dick, then it'll mean you're all right. And maybe they'll ease up on you." They'll ease up from the punishment that they never inflicted. Curious. If you state your own case, it's paranoia; if they state it for you, it becomes social justice.

I would ask you not to judge me on my virtue. I want to work. That speaks for itself. But I want to be judged on my own vision of the world and how I convey it as an artist. Good intentions politically don't necessarily make good art. In fact, beware of good intentions in art. It reminds me of Stanley Kramer, who believes that the message is primary. If you say he's made a bad movie, or that it bored you, he might reply, "Well, you're not pro-Nazi, are you?" The fact is that people who deal in messages primarily, and not in art, are always late. They glorify yesterday's victories, mourn yesterday's victims.

Justice Holmes spoke of a "clear and present danger." The trouble is that most of the "bold" people in the arts perceive the danger to be "clear" only when it is no longer present. Where were the movies about the CIA's killing people, including its own employees, as in *Three Days of the Condor*, five or ten years ago? It's supposedly safe nowadays to admit that the CIA is dangerous, but the current movies don't go beyond that. Garry Wills points out that the predecessor of the CIA, the OSS, was made up of Ivy Leaguers who borrowed from the British imperial tradition of MI6 and who were entirely confident that "good guys" could be licensed killers because they were also gentlemen. Later, we ran out of Ivy Leaguers and had to recruit lower types for the CIA, but the game was the same, although now, as in cricket, there were gentlemen and players. When the CIA turned into an object of Congressional inquiry, and when it was safe for the press to attack it, then the popular artists saw that the danger was now clear but probably no longer present.

So we have *Three Days of the Condor* and *All the President's Men* with Robert Redford, the archetypical American good guy, discovering that the government can kill but, God bless us, the press can absolve. In *Three Days of the Condor*, after Redford's fellow CIA workers have been killed off by their own bosses, guess wherein salvation lies? He's given the story to the New York *Times* in the hope that the whole East Side of New York will know the truth.

Within the restrictions that were imposed, there was, as usual, room for personality. Dan Melnick is now vice president of MGM. When I was in Los Angeles working at Channel 11, Melnick was at Paramount. He drove down to my office and he walked up and put a check down with his name on it, a blank check. And he said, "Fill it in. 'Cause I know you got a problem working." And I said "I don't want that," and he said, "What do you want?" I said, "I want a job." And he said, "I can't give you that."

Joseph Bente of CBS News in L.A. said to me, "Tell your audience that we were in Cambodia two years before Nixon knew about it. The Army went on its own." I said, "Why don't you tell yours; it's a bit more formidable." He said, "Well, I can't, I'm on the air." And he continued to compromise.

Compromise is not what it's cracked up to be. Don't ask Hubert Humphrey to define it for you. Ask Jefferson. You don't get refunds on your conscience: no deposits, no returns. I perceive the liberals in America. Karl Marx never foresaw their role—that the average man conceives his interest to be that of the class to which he aspires. There is no political left in America. The liberals in America are truly the enemies. They were so busy proving that they were not communists, they became totally ineffective.

If I worked on no network at any time—and television broadcasts eighteen hours a day—for ten years, an awful lot of people had to get together. Well, what was it? A conspiracy of two people in a room? Of course not. It was a conspiracy of fear. The key men say no, and the rest know which way the wind blows. When I came on *The Dick Cavett Show*, suddenly Sander Vanocur was booked an hour later so that there would be balance—as if I advocated one side. I never advocated a single or consistent side: I'm anticollectivist. Jack Kennedy said I was in ruthless pursuit of everybody.

This matter of two sides to every question is bad logic and bad practice: sometimes there are no sides; sometimes there are a hundred. When Garrison wrote his book *A Heritage of Stone,* we were booked on *The Steve Allen Show,* and they said there must be a balance—there had to be someone else on. That whole view is absurd. That would mean if Dr. Stillman wants you to diet by drinking ten glasses of water a day, there should be someone on the program who warns against water.

After I was on the radio with a telephone show, the station decided to get away from controversy and put on sports-program shows and young-folks shows, and there's a guy (Elliot Mintz) who told me that when he reported to work at a radio station in L.A., they gave him a handbook for employees that said: "Don't be like Mort Sahl. Don't win the battle and lose the war." Is this an indictment of me? Hitler said that he always knew you could buy the press. What he didn't know was you could get them cheap.

My motivation in defending the honor of President Kennedy was not idealistic. I believed that the people who killed him would be coming for me fifteen minutes later. I'm not eighteen, but I'm the angriest man on any campus I visit. I'm not on the air anymore. I don't have a program. I have myself, but I suppose in terms of modern-day TV and radio that's not considered much of a residual. When I am unemployed, the option to exploit the counterculture does not appeal to me. Because that means saying the entire society stinks and we should all smoke dope. I can never advocate that. What's wrong with the counterculture is that it is safe: the establishment has nothing to fear from it.

Some people said I had no access to audiences because I didn't please them. I never missed with an audience when I was working, and I did not have the benefit of television, where success is instant success. Johnny Carson said that Mort Sahl was fired on television in Los Angeles for boring people with speeches instead of making them laugh. He knows that isn't true, but he's been more unfair to other people. He has Bob Hope on and congratulates him on the trips to Vietnam, but he repeatedly said to me that he found Hope to be a phony patriot who wraps himself in the flag because he wouldn't dare face an audience for fear of failure. (Hope did take his life in his hands, as a matter of fact, going overseas to entertain our boys. I understand the last time he went to Vietnam, his plane was fired at over Berkeley on the way over.)

It's like the time at the Gridiron Club when it held its annual dinner while Nixon was Vice President. Comedians would do everything to try to convulse you. That was the contest. They got to Nixon at the end; they tried everything, and he wouldn't laugh. He didn't laugh. Finally, at the end, the last comedian did the last joke and Nixon laughed. That was the end. On the way out, Nixon turned to Pat Weaver, and Weaver said, "Gee, for a minute there, I didn't think we'd get you." Nixon said, "Off the record, you didn't, but don't you think it was better overall for my image to laugh?" In light of latter-day events, it only hurt when he laughed.

But where were the liberals? Why wasn't their sense of justice offended? Well, perhaps they were mute because their sense of justice had been worn fine. They had given in too many times, had followed too many candidates, had gone to too many conventions and let the candidates pick them. No matter who the Democrats nominate, the liberal's position is, "Well-I-don't-know-who-he-is-but-he-might-work-out." It's reverse English; it's like being pregnant and then trying to fall in love.

We have produced not liberals but social democrats over the last twenty-five years in America. The government produced the CIA, the Dulles brothers produced an arm of the State Department that could activate foreign policy and be unaccountable to the Congress. Sounds too simple? Well, it is as simple as that. It's as simple and as deadly as that. All the forceful, deadly things in the world are simple, as are the successful ones.

When the writers were blacklisted in Hollywood in 1947, was it the fascists who ran them out? Was it Walt Disney and the others? Well, I don't know if they motivated it, but I do know that Dore Schary, the leading liberal light, went to the Waldorf and surrendered to Eric Johnson—it was Appomattox without grace. They purged themselves in the temple.

I remember once when I was at MGM, and a writer and

I were talking about a picture called *How to Make Love in Three Languages.* We idealized the last scene, in which a girl who insists on being an actress falls in love with an analyst. She tears up her Social Security card, throws it into the Trevi Fountain, and decides to be a woman, which is the only decision for a woman to make. Most of them decide to go the other way. Anyway, Abby Mann was upstairs with Stanley Kramer, who always wanted "meaning" in his pictures. My co-writer thought it was a good occasion to go to the studio print shop, where he had printed up a headline that read: SIX MILLION JEWS FOUND ALIVE IN ARGENTINA: ABBY MANN FIRED BY MGM.

Now, we all know that America is the worst country in the world, except for all the others. And we hear people saying that it is beyond redemption. If the system does not work, why would people have to circumvent it with various criminal and espionage activities? We also hear the self-serving explanation that "Watergate may have happened, this national calamity; but if it happened in Russia, it wouldn't have come out." Well, that doesn't help us much, because we have to live here. You can't even get away from your origins. Somebody should tell the Jewish people in Beverly Hills that they're not in the trenches of Israel. (Going to a bond rally is not the same thing, although Steve Allen once said to me, "Jewish people the world over have a common bond." Actually they have a common pledge.)

Americans are stuck with themselves; they only respond differently. We also used to talk about the difference in intellectuals. If a Jewish son differs from his father, he leaves home intellectually. There is much discussion, rationalization, guilt, and anxiety. An Irishman minimizes discussion by punching his father. His father punches him back, and then they go out and get drunk together. But an Italian says to his father, "I'm leaving home forever."

True to his word, he moves out into the back yard and builds his own house.

In addition to the television show, my radio show in Los Angeles had the highest ratings in the city, and the kids who called were the brightest, the most concerned people. Yet I realized that they could easily be anesthetized, as they have been since. They were, underneath that hair, really their fathers. Nonetheless, I tried to nurture them, as I had done the generation before them, and to bring out their dormant humanity. I don't believe in good people and bad people. I believe in the better parts of people. I believe Eugene McCarthy appealed to people because he reminded them what they were like before they were corrupted in Vietnam. And I believe that they have a thorough understanding of Ronald Reagan and Richard Nixon, because they, too, have stared temptation in the face and have not looked away. Look away, look away, look away, fantasyland.

So, I had the telephone show. I was fired after the American people called me and said they were depressed and asked me if what I said was true, and if it was true, was it insurmountable? How do we get rid of the CIA and the generals? I said no, it's not insurmountable. Your own history is against you. You were once an A student, and now you're getting C's. You've got to reapply yourself. To prove my point on the air I suspended the telephone calls and for three hours played the speeches of Franklin D. Roosevelt, because I know the schools don't play them. And I was fired. OK. Now, I'm not Lenny Bruce. I don't think crucifixion is the answer. I believe in the resurrection. I like that part of the story.

One reason to keep going is that the country was given to us as a sacred charge. It is, as Stephen Vincent Benét says in "The Devil and Daniel Webster," not the only place that created a free man—Greece did that—but it is a place

145

that demands that we decide what to do with our freedom. You can only punish yourself. That's the existential view. I don't think there's any reward beyond participating, beyond being here. And the antithesis of reward is punishment, and the only punishment that can come is self-inflicted. I remain optimistic. Whether or not the optimism is justified, I don't know. I want to stay around for the third act. This isn't total darkness; it's just the night approaching.

I learned from William O. Douglas, who in turn learned it from Thomas Jefferson, that the government is to be suspected, that the less government the better, that the police do not need more power. What Warren did all the years he sat on the court with Douglas was to sense what was needed for justice's sake and then ask Douglas to document it constitutionally. Douglas struck a fine balance between the emotion of the times and the equity of all times. That was his humanity. At times I conceived of his standing in Oregon at one end of the country, Fulbright at the other end, holding up the tent for all the rest of us.

Douglas said the most dangerous thing was to be alive. He said "the alive have the most to lose," and he wasn't speaking of life in physical terms only. He came to see me in New York in 1974. It was a heavy conversation. I am going to reveal it because you are to be trusted with what's important to yourself. He came to a New York nightclub. I had sent invitations to the opening in the form of Watergate subpoenas. Douglas walked in and the nightclub captain mistook him for Casey Stengel.

I said, "Mr. Justice, I'm surprised to see you." "No," he said, "you're just surprised that anyone in the government will obey a subpoena." He told me that I must bend every

146

effort to look into the fact that the CIA has a former telephone company executive administering its funds for a
dollar a year and that one of the things he knows about
is that other agencies' funds can be diverted into the CIA.
We talked about other things having to do with the CIA
and he said, "You've got to do it, Mort." I look up, amazed.
He said, "There isn't anybody else." Now, I ask you,
fellow Americans, are you worried now?

At the Democratic Convention in 1972, I spent most of
my time between George Wallace and Gene McCarthy.
I tried to see Shirley Chisholm and was not successful;
and you may have noticed that those stalwarts, the girls
in the Women's Movement, did nothing to help her. The
Women's Movement gives its admiration to Gloria Steinem
and Marlo Thomas and would never have thought to consider that a woman first blew the whistle on the Watergate
crook, because Martha Mitchell wasn't the right stereotype.

McCarthy was once asked by a guy at the *Washington
Post*, "Why do you see Mort Sahl?" McCarthy answered,
"Because we bring out the worst in each other." The press
has presented McCarthy as a global thinker, a forgetful
intellectual. The fact is that he's a forceful intellectual,
and he would be a forceful President. Nixon said that the
press was partisan and was out to get him. He was right.
The architects of the Watergate conspiracy had in mind
a massive shift in power in America. Nixon was offered
up to the press and they took him. Discrediting Nixon was
easy enough, God knows, but how is it you don't see Bern-
stein and Woodward asking about the assassination?

I was hired in 1972 by Katherine Graham to cover
Nixon's inaugural for her *Washington Post* syndicate, and
I attended the inauguration with her. I talked to people
at that paper and I told them what was going on in New
Orleans. And they wouldn't take me on in argument; they
just shook their heads in disbelief that such a thing could

147

happen. Well, it obviously could happen as long as they don't do anything but shake their heads in disbelief. The journalists were supposed to be the potent liberal force.

President Nixon, you know, went to a psychoanalyst, which is not a sign of mental disturbance. It's a sign of a person being intellectually curious about his origins. I admire it; it's an act of bravery. He went to Dr. Walter Hoschnecker. I wonder what Hoschnecker treated Nixon for: was it for lack of humor, for being socially maladaptive, or for being evasive? If so, he should get his money back.

The Democrats had problems too. It was unearthed that Senator Tom Eagleton, the Vice Presidential nominee, had been treated for manic depression by a psychoanalyst, and he was fired by Lawrence O'Brien, who, I understand, said to him, "How dare you be depressed before you've run with Senator McGovern."

In Washington one time, David Brinkley, who is an old friend of mine, invited me to dinner. Bobby Kennedy was there with Ethel and Bob McNamara. My wife was Robert Kennedy's dinner partner, and McNamara was mine. We talked a lot about the TFX, the F-11, and Barry Goldwater. Evans of Evans and Novak was on one side of my wife and Kennedy was on the other. And the conversation was so innocuous that it had to be an effort. Weather was a recurrent topic, and no one ever took a position on it.

I had to leave at eleven o'clock to do a show, and my wife reported that after I left, Kennedy, who continually made pyramids of paper napkins and looked like a man really eaten around the edges, said to her, "Mort said he wrote for my brother. Is that true?" Of course, he knew it was true. Then he said, "Why was he fired from that program in Los Angeles?" Well, I was fired for discussing the assassination of his brother. And it was implicit that if he knew I had a program in California, three thousand miles away, he'd know why. And they continued to pump her for information.

Later, two personal friends of Robert Kennedy, one of whom had been his roommate in college, at the request of the Kennedy family, got in touch with Jim Garrison and attended the preliminary hearing of Clay Shaw. They said that Bobby would wait until he was in a position to be relatively assured of the Presidency and then would get deeper into the case and get the guys who killed Jack. Guys. They used the plural. Garrison said to me later he'll be dead if he wins the California primary. I don't know if Robert Kennedy would have made a choice to listen to a nightclub comedian and a Southern district attorney instead of his brain trust. He never got the opportunity to make that choice.

When I hear people talk of the Irish Mafia and the Boston dealers in pragmatism, I wonder how they found their way into Arlington cemetery. I am alive. I've had a couple of strange car accidents; my back has been broken twice. There have been several attempts made on Garrison's life, but he's intact as far as I know. And our minds are intact. But Jack and Bobby are in Arlington cemetery with the everlasting flame. Is that pragmatism?

Why should you listen to me? Because if you're on my side, you're on the side of life. The current stage of this scenario is for all of us to walk away from Watergate believing that the Presidency does not work, and to have that belief reinforced. That would be the CIA's result, to destroy the Presidency and protect the Company. As I say, that conclusion is reinforced continually by the intellectuals, the Arthur Schlesingers, the McGeorge Bundys, the Ted Sorensens—the ones he trusted. The ones you trusted. But *you're* lucky. You're not in Arlington cemetery.

Remember, a man who believes in something can always defeat one who believes in nothing. That is your great equalizer in this contest. They're here to do their disservice to John Kennedy's legacy because they are the survivors. But you're here to define his legacy. Only you can give it meaning or deny it completely and make it a desert without footprints—as if he were never here. The assignment isn't easy. I'd define it as noble, but I'd never define it as easy. Nothing worthwhile is. And the rewards are bountiful. You're going to get the country back. Look upon my efforts as a lending library. I trust you with the truth and ask you to return it, read and reusable.

We don't live in the same country we were born in. Joseph Heller used the title *Something Happened*. In the '60's we knew that the Pentagon and the Central Intelligence Agency parted company, but then something happened. Like two blips on a traffic controller's screen, the American people and the government (sometimes elected) were converging, and there was no one there to warn them.

I didn't come to the conflict unprepared. My father and mother gave me a very radical orientation. They are people who refused to watch America turn 180 degrees after FDR. But it did turn. Harry Truman was the first President in my time to make cold war America's number-one industry. So when intellectual life was snuffed in Hollywood as a result of the witch hunts; when the United States subsidized Spain, Greece, South Korea, Taiwan, South Vietnam; when the Secretary of Defense became the country's most powerful purchasing agent, then, at that time, the valor in the armed forces was replaced by technocrats.

Something happened. The bogeymen of our youth,

the Joseph Kennedys and the Hearsts—all the barons—
didn't remain as stereotypes opposing government. They
became the government. And some people didn't face it
then! They said things like "Well, Rockefeller at least
won't steal anything—he's too rich," although they had
never in their experience encountered anybody who ever
had *enough* money. Yes, something happened. The enemy
was not going to subjugate the American people; nor was
he going to do what the left told us he would do, which
was to subjugate other people. Rather, he decided to
colonize the last virgin land on earth. He was betting that
we wouldn't mind fourteen years of war in South Vietnam, or that our son's place at the table was empty, because we had exchanged it for a war plant on the corner,
which assured us a Mustang and a second television set
in the bedroom.

So we know where the enemy was. The question is:
Where were our guys? Well, they were having debates in
The New York Review of Books about the machismo of
the President and how it related to invading Asia. Vietnam was never the issue. Vietnam was an object lesson—
the bloodying of Ho Chi Minh's nose would reduce the
crime on our block. We were struggling away to war for
the first time because really we didn't all go together as
in the other wars since the Civil War.

We would never come back the same; some of us would
never come back at all. The war changed the government
at home. The CIA was the most active arm of our foreign
policy and it was not responsible to the Congress. We
had an army dominated by ambivalence and sustained
by narcotics. A generation had gone on a lifetime sit-
down strike. The American dollar was thinning.

No, we didn't live in the country where we were born.
And still there are people who didn't interpret these
events as threatening. They write letters to Ralph Nader

151

when the air conditioner doesn't work. Nader even went so far as to sue an airline when it didn't run on time. Are you listening, Benito Mussolini?

Some of us became so adept at staving off the threat that when the President was murdered and his brother was murdered and Martin Luther King, Jr., was murdered and George Wallace was paralyzed, they scolded the proprietors of hardware stores for selling guns. If you asked them what was the good of it, they said, well, it's a beginning. It's a beginning of the absence of a President, which can only be justified by the absence of a constituency. In place of an inauguration address, the long silence. The shot heard round the world was fired at us.

The protest, ironically, came from unsuspected sources. Instead of minorities saying they weren't being heard, soon no American thought he was being heard. All this was being articulated to me as I flew around the heartland of this country on college tours. It wasn't just blacks, women, and students who were complaining. On airplanes and in waiting rooms, the Rotarian with calculator and legal pad was saying to me that he found the government unresponsive. I took that as a healthy sign. Affirmation. You can't have a real revolution made up of a coalition of farmers and students. You've got to get the folks into it.

When I went out to face the audience, it was no different from a lawyer facing a jury except the composition had now changed. Instead of the Eisenhower audience, which was made up of Democrats who wanted me to attack the Republicans for them, the only rebels for a time were nineteen and under. What I had to say was no longer harmless when I discussed the news. Because the news had grown lethal. Make no mistake. My audience had one helluva time wrestling with the material, because I didn't let them up. It was not by their laughter that I knew them, but by their anger. The anger was proof that they believed me.

So, I beg you. Join the battle for your own sake. Give our existence meaning. Lack of purpose is the worst: it's the insanity with no meaning.

I made a million dollars a year. I emceed the Academy Awards. Then I made just about nothing a year. And I ate coffee and donuts with Jim Garrison. But I felt comradeship. I felt the contribution when I opened Garrison's eyes to the fact that corruption didn't start with Jack Kennedy's murder.

It started with the Cold War gambit. With the reversing and the stripping of gears after Franklin D. Roosevelt. The Marshall Plan. Point Four. The Loyalty Oath. The Defense Department. The Central Intelligence Agency. The ringing of the Soviet Union with missiles. The beginning of a twenty-five-year drunk that ended with people hoping for a merciful Defense Department, and with Ted Kennedy as a hostage.

Jack Anderson reported in his column that Frank Sturgis, one of those burglars indicted in the McGovern headquarters break-in, was a Cuban adventurer who was idealistic about Cuba but always getting into trouble. For instance, continued Anderson, there was even a "crazy rumor" that he was involved in Dealey Plaza and the assassination of President Kennedy. No one checked with Garrison to see if any of those people had been subpoenaed by him but had been denied extradiction to the Orleans Parish during the Clay Shaw trial in 1966 and 1967.

Jack Anderson reported that Ehrlichman and Colson had talked to a sound expert at the CIA who said he could erase the tapes even if they were in another building, through sophisticated equipment. His name: Gordon

Novell. Why did no one in the press check the rumor that E. Howard Hunt had left the country after leaving Dealey Plaza on the day President Kennedy was killed? Why did no one check the correlation between E. Howard Hunt's sending 240 falsified State Department cables attributing the death of Diem to John Kennedy *with* E. Howard Hunt's trip to Chappaquiddick; E. Howard Hunt's being chief of station at the American Embassy at Mexico City when Oswald went there befqre Dallas; as well as the aborted plan to break into Bremer's apartment in Milwaukee to plant a diary explaining Bremer's need to shoot Wallace?

These men had worked at the CIA for twenty-five years. Is anyone naïve enough to think that such men sat there like career firemen waiting for the bell to ring? What kind of house calls did they make in those twenty-five years to advance their expertise? What did Gordon Liddy mean when he said he'd do anything for Nixon? Tell him to assassinate someone, and he'd do it on any street corner. Jack Anderson repeated that Jeb Magruder told Gordon Liddy that they'd have to get rid of Anderson, which meant silence him or throw him off the track. Liddy organized the Cuban assassination team to get rid of him.

In 1971 and 1972 all avenues were cut off to me except the colleges. I must have played five hundred. All those students! All that travel! All that hair! After a show at Niagara Falls Community College, there was a reception hosted by a faculty adviser who won Godzilla on *The Dating Game*. They served coffee and cookies—spiked with acid. I received a call advising me my mother had had multiple strokes in L.A., and since I had just been given a car, I started driving.

I lost spatial perception first. Headlights appeared to be motorcycles converging from 180-degree angles. The road surface was magnified. I saw a whale and the white line was the tongue I was driving down. After three days, China called Garrison, who alerted the highway patrols cross-country. I called her from Albuquerque. "I'll be home soon. I just saw myself drive away." Objective detachment—great in critics.

I woke up with my arms at my sides going over the side in New Mexico into a canyon—at fifty-five I heard my back break. I drove out of the hole and got to Winslow, Arizona, where I stopped because I thought I saw Marines in a landing rope on the side of a ship which turned out to be a freight car. Two cops grabbed me (with drawn guns) and busted me for drugs. "Hollywood. Look at the beard. Flowered shirt." No-doz on the seat for evidence. The arm of a black T-shirt sticking out of a laundry bag I mistook for China's profile, her hairline, and I conversed with it for three days. They took me to a hospital and never looked at my back, not for six hours. I remember that the doctors talked about how Jews go into medicine for money. The doctor told the police he would not verify the presence of narcotics. "Extreme fatigue." They told me I had to go to sleep. The Travelodge was across the street (twelve bucks). "You have to sleep here (the hospital) and vacate the bed at 8:00 (it's 2:00 A.M.) (sixty-five bucks). They impounded the car. When the cops' shift ended, the doc sprung me, and I took a cab 150 miles to Phoenix.

I went into a brace for one year, the Arizona police stole my clothes, and I accused them on *The Dick Cavett Show*. The Commander wrote me and assured me Arizona police were as honest as any other—unquote. Three doctors diagnosed LSD in my system. I read the other day about the CIA using acid. Of course, now it's not paranoia to talk about it.

On my new television show, in early 1975, Robert

155

Vaughan appeared to plead for a reopening of the Robert Kennedy case. I remember dining with him ten years before and when I asked the waiter why my order was delayed, Vaughan answered: "Maybe the long arm of the CIA has reached into the kitchen." I stood up with clenched fists. "Stand up and get your time, you son of a bitch."

"Don't get sore. It's a joke. I didn't know you felt so strongly."

"I don't mind that the sum of my life is a momentary joke for your amusement. That's more meaning than you've assigned to death since it was perpetrated," I told him.

Two of my old friends in the press corps were Merriman Smith, chief of White House scribes, and Chuck Roberts of *Newsweek*. Roberts wrote a book titled *The Truth About the Assassination*. That's a handy guide if the contents don't help you. Smitty won a Pulitzer Prize for describing Kennedy alive in the car going under the underpass, when in fact he died before he reached it. Smitty was extremely happy-go-lucky—right up until the day he shot himself.

How many more have to die before some Americans realize murder is not a way of life? Too many have lost America because they brought her their lust, but could never love her. For one, Hugh Hefner, who is now reduced to attacking Mae Brussells, who is an assassination researcher who pursues the murders among us selflessly. What did Garfield say in *Body and Soul*? What are you gonna do? Kill me? Everybody dies. Hefner sent a prominent novelist to ordain her a paranoid. America's poet laureate, Don McLean, reminds us, "Just because you're paranoid doesn't mean they're not out to get you." Writers? Well, Mark Harris says the greatest danger to America is people who see assassins, not assassins themselves. Twelve years ago, no less, Jean Stafford showed us a mad Marguerite Oswald. So we know we can't count on the intellectuals. Like the Hollywood Ten, they discovered a lack of interest in their country *after* they went to jail.

And I started the battle early. The enemy isn't political in nature. It's insanity, which I combatted through purpose. But even Kafka couldn't envision that the enemy would become apathy. I learned a little along the way: the bad times, the years in the foxholes. An introduction to the devil does not constitute equal opportunity.

We've gone from Henry Wallace to Spiro Agnew.

We've gone from Jefferson to Ford.

From Roosevelt, Churchill, and Stalin to Ford, Brezhnev, and Wilson.

From Paul Muni to Burt Reynolds.

From Oscar Wilde to Gore Vidal.

From purpose to anticommunism.

From love to indifference.

Darwin was wrong.

Is it too late for America? How many lies before you belong to the lies? You can't return to your own lines. They don't recognize you. You are made different by the company you keep. Nixon reminds you of what you have become. McCarthy reminds you of who you were.

I'm relaxing now from my monastic writing chores. I'm watching Merv Griffin speaking to James Whitmore, who's appearing in a one-man show: George Plimpton. Whitmore has been Truman as well as Will Rogers. He and Will, Jr., agree that Will was "not like Mort Sahl. His humor never hurt." Let sleeping Presidents lie. In fact, let living Presidents lie.

My story isn't special but it's strenuous. I took America at its word. We were right and we were wrong. We were right to pursue the murderers among us. We were in error in pleading the case for America in Beverly Hills and New York. Here reside the phrases "I can't bring myself to believe" and "I loved him so much it's too painful." Don't appeal to the intellectuals. The hope of America is the heartland.

Now you know there are murderers among us, killers of the dream. You know what they did. I know some of you don't want to get involved, but you began your involvement when you began life.

Do it for the best friend you ever had, John F. Kennedy. Do it for yourself.

You must do it, because there is no one else.

Don't be diverted by prefab threats. Wallace is painted a lunatic, but why does he appeal? He's anti-elitest, for one thing, and he has had enough courage to examine the attempt on his life. For that matter, the populist suspicion of the federal government is maybe what stands between you and an unstated fascism now.

I tried to answer your questions. Now I have two. Is anybody listening? Does anybody care?